D1826105

Mobility, Education and Life Trajectories

Migration for educational purposes, once the privilege of the upper class, has become a global mass phenomenon in recent years. This volume examines, within different cultural and historical contexts, the close relationship between migration, education, and social mobility. Adopting the perspective that education includes a broad range of formative experiences, the chapters explore different educational trajectories and the local, regional, and transnational relations in which they are embedded. Three key issues emerge from the analyses: firstly, the central role of temporal aspects in terms of both the overall historical conditions and the specific biographical circumstances shaping educational opportunities; secondly, the complex agendas informing individuals' migration and the adjustment of these agendas in the light of the vagaries of migrant life; and thirdly, the importance of migrants' self-perception as 'educated persons', and the invention of new identities, and the maintaining of old identities that this involves.

This book was originally published as a special issue of *Identities: Global Studies in Culture and Power.*

Karen Valentin is Associate Professor in the Department of Educational Anthropology, School of Education, at Aarhus University, Denmark. Her research areas are education, migration, urban life, and youth, based on fieldwork in Nepal, India, Vietnam, and Denmark.

Karen Fog Olwig is Professor in the Department of Anthropology at the University of Copenhagen, Denmark. Her research has focused on the significance of family and kinship in processes of migration, in both a Caribbean and a Danish context.

Mobility, Education and Life Trajectories

New and old migratory pathways

Edited by

Karen Valentin and Karen Fog Olwig

Taylor & Francis Group

LONDON AND NEW YORK

First published 2017
by Routledge

2 Park Square, Milton Park, Abingdon, Oxfordshire OX14 4RN
711 Third Avenue, New York, NY 10017

Routledge is an imprint of the Taylor & Francis Group, an informa business

First issued in paperback 2018

British Library Cataloguing in Publication Data
A catalogue record for this book is available from the British Library

ISBN: 978-1-138-20230-6 (hbk)
ISBN: 978-0-367-02899-2 (pbk)

Typeset in Times New Roman
by RefineCatch Limited, Bungay, Suffolk

Publisher's Note
The publisher accepts responsibility for any inconsistencies that may have
arisen during the conversion of this book from journal articles to book chapters,
namely the possible inclusion of journal terminology.

Disclaimer
Every effort has been made to contact copyright holders for their permission to
reprint material in this book. The publishers would be grateful to hear from any
copyright holder who is not here acknowledged and will undertake to rectify
any errors or omissions in future editions of this book.

Contents

Citation Information

The chapters in this book were originally published in *Identities: Global Studies in Culture and Power*, volume 22, issue 3 (June 2015). When citing this material, please use the original page numbering for each article, as follows:

Chapter 1
Mobility, education and life trajectories: new and old migratory pathways
Karen Fog Olwig and Karen Valentin
Identities: Global Studies in Culture and Power, volume 22, issue 3
(June 2015), pp. 247–257

Chapter 2
Migrating for a profession: becoming a Caribbean nurse in post-WWII Britain
Karen Fog Olwig
Identities: Global Studies in Culture and Power, volume 22, issue 3
(June 2015), pp. 258–272

Chapter 3
Rescuing children, reforming the Empire: British child migration to colonial Southern Rhodesia
Katja Uusihakala
Identities: Global Studies in Culture and Power, volume 22, issue 3
(June 2015), pp. 273–287

Chapter 4
Gendered educational trajectories and transnational marriage among West African students in France
Hélène Neveu Kringelbach
Identities: Global Studies in Culture and Power, volume 22, issue 3
(June 2015), pp. 288–302

CITATION INFORMATION

Chapter 5
'La Lenin is my passport': schooling, mobility and belonging in socialist Cuba and its diaspora
Mette Louise Berg
Identities: Global Studies in Culture and Power, volume 22, issue 3 (June 2015), pp. 303–317

Chapter 6
Transnational education and the remaking of social identity: Nepalese student migration to Denmark
Karen Valentin
Identities: Global Studies in Culture and Power, volume 22, issue 3 (June 2015), pp. 318–332

Chapter 7
Becoming independent through au pair migration: self-making and social re-positioning among young Filipinas in Denmark
Karina Märcher Dalgas
Identities: Global Studies in Culture and Power, volume 22, issue 3 (June 2015), pp. 333–346

Chapter 8
Converting experiences in 'communities of practice': 'educational' migration in Denmark and achievements of Ukrainian agricultural apprentices
Vera Skvirskaja
Identities: Global Studies in Culture and Power, volume 22, issue 3 (June 2015), pp. 347–361

For any permission-related enquiries please visit:
http://www.tandfonline.com/page/help/permissions

Notes on Contributors

Mette Louise Berg is Senior Lecturer in the Thomas Coram Research Unit, Department of Social Science, University College London, UK.

Karina Märcher Dalgas is Research Fellow at the Department of Anthropology, University of Copenhagen, Denmark.

Hélène Neveu Kringelbach is Lecturer in African Studies, University College London, UK.

Karen Fog Olwig is Professor in the Department of Anthropology, University of Copenhagen, Denmark.

Vera Skvirskaja is Associate Professor in the Department of Cross-Cultural and Regional Studies, University of Copenhagen, Denmark.

Katja Uusihakala is Academy Research Fellow in the Department of Social and Cultural Anthropology, University of Helsinki, Finland.

Karen Valentin is Associate Professor in the Department of Educational Anthropology, School of Education, Aarhus University, Denmark.

Mobility, education and life trajectories: new and old migratory pathways

Karen Fog Olwig and Karen Valentin

Travel for educational purposes, once the privilege of the upper class, has become a global mass phenomenon in recent years. This special issue examines, within different cultural and historical contexts, the close relation ship between migration, education and social mobility. Adopting the per spective that education includes a broad range of formative experiences, the articles explore different educational trajectories and the local, regional and transnational relations in which they are embedded. Three key issues emerge from the analyses: firstly, the central role of temporality in terms of both the overall historical conditions and the specific biographical circumstances shaping educational opportunities; secondly, the complex agendas informing individuals' migration and the adjustment of these agendas in the light of the vagaries of migrant life; and thirdly, the importance of migrants' self percep tion as 'educated persons' and the invention of new, and the maintaining of old, identities that this involves.

Migration for educational purposes has become a global mass phenomenon. Some young people travel as bona fide students who have been accepted at institutions of formal education, making such places of instruction their official gateway to life in a new society. Yet, these young people must often engage in extensive wage employment in order to support themselves and possibly also their families, who may have contributed substantially to financing their trip abroad. Others move as part of various educational, professional or cultural exchange programmes, as, for example, interns or au pairs. While the latter may have less explicitly defined educational goals, many seek to carve out longer-term educational trajectories that enable them to stay on and use education as a stepping stone to furthering their careers abroad.

This special issue explores the varying trajectories associated with educa-tional migration, the local, regional and transnational relations in which it has been embedded at different historical conjunctures and the assertion of new and old identities with which it is linked. Acknowledging that education is not limited to standardised, institutionalised forms of learning, but encompasses other for-mative experiences as well, the special issue takes its point of departure in the idea that migration itself involves learning processes and that an important aspect

1

of the migration experience is becoming skilful at navigating in different, uncertain and structurally constrained learning and work environments (Rao and Hossain 2012; Valentin 2012; Hertrich and Lesclingand 2013). By adopting a broad understanding of education, it is thus possible to explore, first, how education may attain multiple and shifting meanings depending on the social context and individual life circumstances and on whether it entails school-based learning or other socially situated forms of learning (Lave and Wenger 1991; Levinson 1999), and secondly, how disparate learning paths are interwoven into, and shape, livelihood opportunities (Froerer and Portisch 2012). This issue takes this approach one step further by specifically exploring, from a cross-cultural perspective, the role of education in the interrelated processes of geographical and social mobility.

Bridging migration research and educational anthropology through educational migration

Addressing the issue of mobility from three different perspectives – geographical movements, educational processes and shifts in social status – and the interconnectedness between them in individual trajectories, this volume aims to bridge discussions from the field of migration studies with those of educational anthropology. Although there have been few attempts to conceptualise the role of education in geographical mobility, the relationship between migration and education figures as a theme in the literature in at least three different ways.

Firstly, especially in societies with a long history of immigration, such as the United States, there is a well-established tradition of examining how schools endeavour to turn migrants' children into new citizens. The field of educational anthropology, with its roots in studies of American minority education (Levinson and Holland 1996), has thus long been preoccupied with issues of social inequality and reproduction in relation to the descendants of migrants. It has primarily adopted an institutional perspective focusing on the role of schools in incorporating immigrants into receiving societies. Particularly, important issues have been whether schools serve as avenues of social and economic mobility or essentially (re)produce existing ethnic and racial structures of social and economic differentiation, as well as immigrants' own strategies of integration in relation to school educational programmes (see, for example, Ogbu and Simons 1998; Waters 1999; Gibson and Koyama 2011). While ideas of mobility (often perceived of and represented as a lack of mobility due to socially and socioeconomically exclusive education systems) are central to this body of literature, it examines mobility mainly within status hierarchies in the receiving society rather than geographical mobility practices involving education, broadly defined, as one of many pathways towards social mobility. Furthermore, it has paid little attention to migrants' lives and mobility practices prior to international migration.

Secondly, from a historical perspective, there has been an interest in the significance of travel abroad for educational purposes in the more advantaged segments of society. For many years, study abroad was viewed as the privilege of a small, select group of young people who were able to travel for educational purposes because they either had wealthy parents or were the fortunate recipients of scholarships. This mobility enabled them to gain the professional and intellectual skills necessary to maintain a particular livelihood, but also – in the tradition of the Grand Tour – the social and cultural skills associated with upper- or middle-class life. Research has therefore pointed to the key role of travel in the cultural reproduction of the wealthy elite and the production of a professional middle class (Towner 1985; Henry 2002; Olwig 2007). In a recent work, Amit (2010) has noted that international student exchanges at Western universities, which have been expanded and institutionalised through formal exchange programmes in recent decades, are often regarded as a continuation of the Grand Tour because they are believed to facilitate the acquisition of important language and cultural skills. They, therefore, tend to be viewed as an unquestioned good, and there has been little critical research within this area of study (but see, for example, Amit and Dyck 2010).

Thirdly, of late, as the rapid growth in student migration from postcolonial or postsocialist societies has become more and more apparent, there has been increasing interest in the role of education in international population movements. Contributions from, among others, human geographers have examined the significance of both geographical and social mobility and have explored the spatial differentiation and fundamentally unequal structures governing international student mobility (Brooks and Waters 2011). Migration researchers have mainly directed their attention towards the mobility of students of modest financial means who are enrolling in a wide variety of educational, cultural exchange and intern programmes abroad. We suggest that this form of mobility for educational purposes may have attracted particular interest because it can be viewed as a new form of migration by disadvantaged people looking for opportunities in the Western world, the traditional topic of interest in migration studies. Studies have therefore generally centred on issues that have been salient in research on labour migration, such as the impact of visa regulations on migration flows and the exploitation of immigrants. Key topics include, on the one hand, the use of student visas as a means of gaining entrance to attractive migration destinations and, on the other, the exploitation of international students as a cheap source of labour in the receiving societies and the questionable quality of many of the available educational and cultural programmes that seem designed primarily to take advantage of the economic potential of this new student population (see, for example, Baas 2006, 2009; Fleischer 2007; Neilson 2009; Hassam 2010; Búrikocá and Miller 2010; Pan 2011).

The contributions in this volume draw on these different approaches in research on the relationship between education and migration. Thus, they acknowledge the role of educational institutions in the creation of new citizens, the significance of cultural, social and professional skills acquired abroad in the (re)production of class and the exploitative structures encountered by students who often enter a foreign country with limited legal rights and financial resources. At the same time, the articles recognise that migrants may understand and interpret experiences abroad in many different ways. Furthermore, in the face of difficulties, which may seem to make them victims of structures of oppression, they will generally endeavour to make the best of the opportunities that arise and engage in pursuits and relationships that they find meaningful. And when routes of expected educational and social mobility turn into dead ends, they rework social positions and related identities and explore alternative paths of opportunity. The aim of this issue is to focus on these subject-oriented dimensions of mobility as well as the objective structural conditions that impact on their mobility. This means paying attention to the migrants' perceptions of, and practices in relation to, educational achievement and social status, how they develop through time and how as a consequence of various changes migrants construct new identities or seek to maintain old ones as 'educated persons' worthy of social recognition in the country of origin as well as in the society of the migration destination. Basic to this approach is a broad understanding of the notion of education.

Educational trajectories and mobile livelihoods

From an anthropological perspective, education is not just school-based learning but includes a wide range of socially legitimate processes of training and learning whereby members of a given society come to define themselves and become recognised as knowledgeable and educated according to specific cultural criteria (Levinson and Holland 1996). Taking on multiple and shifting meanings depending on context and situation, education is not identical with, but encompasses, the formal system of schooling. This system has been an integral part of the formation of colonial and postcolonial societies as well as the development of the nation state as a political form (Fuller 1991). Education has also played a key role throughout the world as a mode of social and economic mobility for those aspiring to middle-class status, as testified by studies of migration in relation to the late colonial or postcolonial worlds, or educational programmes in socialist areas of the world.

The global expansion of modern schooling in the second half of the twentieth century was inextricably linked with prevailing modernistic ideas of a positive correlation between mass schooling, economic progress and national development (Anderson-Levitt 2003). This has resulted in huge expectations of the transformative potential of formal education on both the societal and individual levels. The growth in educational migration throughout the world can also be seen as an aspect of contemporary processes of globalisation that lead institutions in the Global North to recruit young trainees and students abroad and encourage young people to seek educational opportunities abroad. At a more general level, education is also an integral dimension of the mobile livelihoods and transnational networks of relations that have been important for people in the developing and postsocialist worlds who see limited future prospects in their home countries.

The notion of livelihood (Olwig and Sørensen 2002) concerns not only obtaining the necessary material means of subsistence but just as significantly fulfilling the ambition to achieve culturally conditioned goals regarding desirable occupations and modes of living. Often, however, such ambitions cannot be realised within the confines of the local society or the nation state, and they may therefore lead to extensive physical mobility, resulting in mobile livelihoods. Young people who leave for an education abroad thus arrive with well-defined ideas of what kinds of livelihoods, and associated social and economic mobility, they expect their physical mobility will facilitate. Such ambitions may be entirely unrealistic given the opportunities available to temporary educational migrants. International research has shown, however, that it can be difficult for migrants to downscale their goals because they are embedded in transnational social networks that maintain high expectations of migrants' achievements abroad (Fleischer 2007; Olwig 2007). Important elements in these social networks are the migrants' economic and social obligations towards relatives and friends who have helped finance and organise their migration, as well as their emotional ties to their country of origin, where they anticipate returning when they have achieved the desired social mobility. Migrants thus struggle for geographical and social mobility within a complex field of contradictory expectations and demands. They are regarded as key resources in the transnational networks of relations extending to family and friends in their country of origin and abroad, while treated as foreigners in the migration destination and being subjected to tight immigration regulations that may stake out a limited space of opportunity. In this special issue we investigate how this contested social arena restricts migrants' ability to strive for social and economic mobility and the various ways in which they seek to deal with, or circumvent, these limitations.

Major themes

This special issue examines the role of education – ranging from primary and secondary schooling to higher education, to training for a profession, to participating in an agricultural internship and to being immersed in the culture and language of a foreign country – as an integrated part of the livelihood strategies of the migrants and their families and the hopes and ambitions for social and geographical mobility linked to these strategies. The articles focus on key themes in the field of educational migration and their relevance for questions of social identity formation. The first two articles apply a primarily historical perspective by looking at educational migration through the lens of colonial ties. The articles on the training of Caribbean nurses in the United Kingdom (Olwig) and on the migration of British children to Southern Rhodesia (Uusihakala) analyse two very different kinds of educational migration within the British Empire during the late colonial period. With a focus on migration from Senegal to France, the third article examines the relationship between educational migration and transnational marriage in the former French Empire (Neveu Kringelbach). All three articles highlight the key role of education as a means of creating 'proper' colonial subjects, the migratory moves between the colonies and the imperial centres in which this resulted, and how migrants have experienced these moves. The next article (Berg), on alumni from an elite school in socialist Cuba, is also concerned with education as a state project. It discusses the physical and social mobility with which it is associated and points to the importance of social networks and elite identities in the formation of an 'alumni-based' diaspora. The remaining articles explore three different kinds of contemporary educational migration to Denmark: Nepalese studying at institutions of higher education (Valentin), Filipina au pairs on cultural exchanges in private homes (Dalgas) and Ukrainian apprentices on farms (Skvirskaja). They emphasise both how aspirations for social and economic mobility are intertwined with desires for personal transformation and how individuals' social identities are continuously being remade in processes of migration. In the following, we discuss three major cross-cutting themes that emerge from the articles.

Temporality

With their focus on the relationship between mobility and education, the articles highlight the key role of temporality in migration processes in terms of both the overall historical conditions and the more specific biographical circumstances that shape migration. The case studies point to the significance of the broader political, economic and institutional context within which specific, culturally conditioned ideas of the educated person emerge and become associated with certain social statuses and relations of power that may lead to migration for educational purposes. The migration of Caribbean student nurses to Britain, of British children to Rhodesia and of young Senegalese to France are all outcomes of colonial relations and closely linked to the production of the particular sorts of colonial subject that these relations involved. This political project has resulted in the emergence of well-established migratory routes to imperial centres of learning that are still prominent, even after the political ties have changed character. We find a similar political project, albeit within a different historical context and on a smaller geographical scale, in the move of bright Cuban children from their home to elite boarding schools with the aim of producing loyal citizens of the young communist state. Educational migration to Denmark from Nepal, the Philippines and Ukraine, on the other hand, involves pathways that have emerged in recent years, largely as responses to time-specific political demands for the internationalisation of education and the liberalisation of labour markets, offering opportunities for new categories of migrants.

Most of the articles examine experiences of educational migration in retrospect – as 'turning points' in individual life courses (Brettell 2002) that have had significant implications for future lives. From a life-history perspective, a focus on educational migration inevitably draws our attention to the formative years of childhood and youth. The articles show that not only formal education abroad but also travel away from home has a great impact on young migrants. They also demonstrate how migrants, in turn, may use their experiences abroad to claim certain positions, whether as independent, respected adult members of the family and the local community, as in the case of the Filipina au pairs, or as socially recognised members of the middle class in the case of the Nepalese students or Caribbean student nurses. The importance of the formative dimension of migration is further underlined by the fact that migration for educational purposes often takes place at a point in life, when young people are seeking to establish their own families. Whether they find spouses abroad (as exemplified by the Senegalese students), or bring spouses from home (as is the case with the Nepalese students), marriage practices can have an important impact on their educational opportunities and the life trajectories they open up.

Complexity

The educational programmes examined here involve well-defined rules, guidelines and purposes, sanctioned by the countries involved, whether they concern children's schooling, further education for adults, the training of apprentices or general cultural enrichment. Within this official framework, however, participants can be seen to have pursued a variety of agendas. For the young movers, strong driving forces – apart from the desire to explore educational opportunities – include the possibility of experiencing adventure and acquiring knowledge of the world, gaining access to attractive wage employment abroad or just getting away and avoiding the negative identity of being 'stagnant', 'stuck' or a 'standby' who is making no progress in life. For young women, especially, an important appeal of educational migration is also its image as a socially legitimate way to leave home that enables freedom and independence of a kind that would have been impossible had they stayed at home. For the family, in turn, educational migration is often associated with expectations of receiving remittances and benefiting from the social prestige enjoyed by having an educated person in one's family.

Young people experience a similarly wide spectrum of more or less explicit agendas in the educational programmes. They meet serious institutions concerned with offering the best education, ideological programmes intent on turning children and young people into good national or colonial subjects, entrepreneurial schemes looking for easy profit, and designs to obtain a willing and inexpensive labour force for unpopular jobs in the receiving society – often in various combinations. Some young people get hopelessly bogged down in this mire of disparate, if not conflicting intentions, obligations, hopes and desires associated with educational programmes. A good proportion of the British children who attended boarding school in Rhodesia simply felt abandoned by their families, while many of the Cuban children enjoyed their elite education, but rejected the larger political project of which it was part. For both groups, further migration became the best option. Many of the adult educational migrants found it difficult to live up to the great social and economic expectations associated with their stay abroad while managing the excessive workload necessary to fund their studies and dealing with the vagaries of life in a foreign country. However, being well educated and therefore relatively resourceful and self-confident, they made the best of the opportunities available to them, using the skills, connections and income acquired through their educational exposure to improve their social and economic status at home and abroad.

Identities and the educated person

Because of the varying historical and personal circumstances under which educational migration takes place and the many different agendas that may be associated with it, it can generate a variety of social identities, both self-ascribed and ascribed by others. Educational migration as such is linked to a student identity that, in general, is imbued with hopes and future prospects for social recognition. Far from all, however, travel along well-defined educational routes. The Nepalese students and many of the Senegalese youths need to engage in extensive wage employment in order to underwrite their studies. They, therefore, risk becoming identified as unskilled foreign workers, a status they reject, for example, by engaging in associations abroad that can confirm their student status, by redefining their notion of a student identity and by concealing the extensive work experiences they had abroad when they return.

Some migrants, however, do not identify with the educational aims of the programme that facilitated their migration. Many, if not most of the graduates from La Lenin, rejected the identities associated with the political ideology that shaped their school in Cuba, and the participants in the Fairbridge scheme in Rhodesia were, retrospectively, critical of the felt lack of adult care and presence in their lives, as well as the harsh discipline they experienced in the boarding school. Students from both schools, however, developed a strong sense of belonging grounded in relationships with the peers who shared the same educational experiences. These relationships became the basis of strong transnational networks providing an important source of identity for those who migrated. Similar notions of identification, based on peer relations developed abroad, emerged among the Caribbean, Nepalese and Senegalese educational migrants and helped them broaden their understanding of their social identity as educated persons. Migration for educational purposes therefore involves continuous shifts in social positioning and the negotiation of several social identities that, at times, can be experienced as conflicting, but also as liberating.

The ambiguity of identities associated with educational migration is perhaps most marked in the case of the Filipina au pairs, Ukrainian trainees and Caribbean student nurses whose participation in educational programmes is closely linked to the recruitment of foreign labour. In this case, the formal student identity in the receiving society often comes to be eclipsed by the socially ascribed identity of being a foreign, racialised labour force performing the dirty, badly paid work that the local population is not willing to do. There is a risk that research, which is primarily concerned with the exploitative dimensions of educational migration, may unwittingly contribute to reinforcing this negative image of these migrants. It is, of course, of great importance to point to these problems, which may lead to downward social and economic mobility and a loss of self-esteem among the young migrants. It is equally crucial, however, to have an eye for the social networks, cultural competences and forms of personal development that may be engendered by migration for educational purposes. By focusing on these dimensions of educational migration and the variegated social identities associated with them, this special issue sheds light on an important aspect of educational migration that so far has received little attention.

Conclusion

By putting mobility in the centre of analysis, this special issue on educational migration offers a timely contribution both to migration studies and to the field of educational anthropology. While the relationship between education and migration has been addressed in previous studies examining such topics as the role of education in the incorporation of immigrants into host societies, the explorative dimensions of youth travel and the overlapping spheres of educational and labour migration, relatively little attention has been paid to the significance of mobility as such in these processes. This issue of educational migration, thus, opens up for exploration of the complexities and interrelatedness of different forms of mobility, which can enrich both migration and education studies. The articles demonstrate the varying configurations, purposes and meanings this particular form of population movement can take. More specifically, they point to the importance of the general historical conditions as well as the more specific biographical circumstances that shape migration, the range of individual and family-based agendas that may be involved in the educational project, and the ambiguity of the identities and the associated subjectivities negotiated by the migrants. At a more general level, they therefore underscore the need to recognise that migration, as an integral aspect of human life, cannot be fully grasped when viewed primarily as a result of global structures of inequality, but needs to be grounded in in-depth case studies that can reveal the complexity and agency of the lives that it involves.

References

Amit, V. 2010. "Student Mobility and Internationalisation: Rationales, Rhetoric and 'Institutional Isomorphism'." *Anthropology in Action* 17 (1): 6 18. doi:10.3167/aia.2010.170102.

Amit, V., and N. Dyck. 2010. "Unsystematic Systems." *Anthropology in Action* 17 (1): 1 5. doi:10.3167/aia.2010.170101.

Anderson Levitt, K. 2003. "A World Culture of Schooling?" In *Local Meanings, Global Schooling: Anthropology and World Culture Theory*, edited by K. Anderson Levitt, 1 16. New York: Palgrave Macmillan.

Baas, M. 2006. "Cash Cows. Milking Indian Students in Australia." *IIAS Newsletter* 42: 14.

Baas, M. 2009. "Curry Bashing: Racism, Violence and Alien Space Invaders." *Economic & Political Weekly XLIV* 34: 37 42.

Brettell, C. 2002. "Gendered Lives: Transitions and Turning Points in Personal, Family, and Historical Time." *Current Anthropology* 43: S45 S61. doi:10.1086/339565.

Brooks, R., and J. Waters. 2011. *Student Mobilities, Migration and the Internationalization of Higher Education*. London: Palgrave Macmillan.

Búriková, Z., and D. Daniel Miller. 2010. *Au Pair*. Cambridge: Polity Press.

Fleischer, A. 2007. "Family, Obligations, and Migration: The Role of Kinship in Cameroon." *Demographic Research* 16 (13): 413 440. doi:10.4054/DemRes.2007.16.13.

Froerer, P., and A. Portisch. 2012. "Introduction to the Special Issue: Learning, Livelihoods, and Social Mobility." *Anthropology and Education Quarterly* 43 (4): 332 343. doi:10.1111/j.1548 1492.2012.01188.x.

Fuller, B. 1991. *Growing Up Modern: The Western State Builds Third World Schools*. New York: Routledge.

Gibson, M. A., and J. P. Koyama. 2011. "Immigrants and Education." In *A Companion to the Anthropology of Education*, edited by B. A. U. Levinson and M. Pollock, 391 407. West Sussex: Wiley Blackwell.

Hassam, A. 2010. "Salaam Namaste, Melbourne and Cosmopolitanism." In *Bollywood in Australia: Transnationalism and Cultural Production*, edited by A. Hassam and M. Paranjape, 63 86. Crawley, WA: UWA.

Henry, M. A. 2002. "The Making of Elite Culture." In *A Companion to Eighteenth Century Britain*, edited by H. T. Dickingson, 311 328. London: Blackwell Publishers.

Hertrich, V., and M. Lesclingand. 2013. "Adolescent Migration in Rural Africa as a Challenge to Gender and Intergenerational Relationships: Evidence from Mali." *The ANNALS of the American Academy of Political and Social Science* 648 (1): 175 188. doi:10.1177/0002716213485356.

Lave, J., and E. Wenger. 1991. *Situated Learning: Legitimate Peripheral Participation*. Cambridge: Cambridge University Press.

Levinson, B. A. 1999. "Resituating the Place of Educational Discourse in Anthropology." *American Anthropologist* 101 (3): 594 604. doi:10.1525/aa.1999.101.3.594.

Levinson, B. A., and D. C. Holland. 1996. "The Cultural Production of the Educated Person: An Introduction." In *The Cultural Production of the Educated Person: Critical Ethnographies of Schooling and Local Practice*, edited by B. A. Levinson, D. E. Foley, and D. C. Holland, 1 54. Albany, NY: SUNY Press.

Neilson, B. 2009. "The World Seen from a Taxi: Students Migrants Workers in the Global Multiplication of Labour." *Subjectivity* 29 (1): 425 444. doi:10.1057/sub.2009.23.

Ogbu, J. U., and H. D. Simons. 1998. "Voluntary and Involuntary Minorities: A Cultural Ecological Theory of School Performance with Some Implications for Education." *Anthropology & Education Quarterly* 29 (2): 155 188. doi:10.1525/aeq.1998.29.2.155.

Olwig, K. F. 2007. *Caribbean Journeys: An Ethnography of Migration and Home in Three Family Networks*. Durham, NC: Duke University Press.

Olwig, K. F., and N. N. Sørensen. 2002. "Mobile Livelihoods: Making a Living in the World." In *Work and Migration. Life and Livelihoods in a Globalizing World*, edited by N. N. Sørensen and K. F. Olwig, 1 19. London: Routledge.

Pan, D. 2011. "Student Visas, Undocumented Labour, and the Boundaries of Legality: Chinese Migration and English as a Foreign Language Education in the Republic of Ireland." *Social Anthropology* 19 (3): 268 287. doi:10.1111/j.1469 8676.2011.00159.x.

Rao, N., and M. I. Hossain. 2012. "'I Want to Be Respected': Migration, Mobility, and the Construction of Alternate Educational Discourses in Rural Bangladesh." *Anthropology and Education Quarterly* 43 (4): 415 428. doi:10.1111/j.1548 1492.2012.01194.x.

Towner, J. 1985. "The Grand Tour: A Key Phase in the History of Tourism." *Annals of Tourism Research* 12: 297 333. doi:10.1016/0160 7383(85)90002 7.

Valentin, K. 2012. "The Role of Education in Mobile Livelihoods: Social and Geographical Routes of Young Nepalese Migrants in India." *Anthropology and Education Quarterly* 43 (4): 429 442. doi:10.1111/j.1548 1492.2012.01195.x.

Waters, M. 1999. *Black Identities: West Indian Immigrant Dreams and American Realities*. Cambridge, MA: Harvard University Press.

Migrating for a profession: becoming a Caribbean nurse in post-WWII Britain

Karen Fog Olwig

Youths from the Global South migrating for further education often face various forms of discrimination. This Caribbean case study discusses how conditions in the home country can provide a foundation for educational migration that helps the migrants overcome such obstacles and even develop a strong sense of agency and self empowerment. In the post WWII period, numerous Caribbean women trained in nursing at British hospitals that have been described as marred by race and gender related inequality and asso ciated forms of exploitation. Yet, the nurses interviewed about this training emphasised its high quality and downplayed the problems encountered. This positive attitude, it is argued, must be understood in the light of the key ideological role of education, particularly for a profession, as an avenue of social and personal mobility in the late colonial Caribbean societies and the ways in which it enabled these Caribbean women to stake out a new life for themselves.

Introduction

During the post-WWII period, British officials began recruiting student nurses overseas to fill the great need for hospital staff after the establishment of the British National Health Service in 1948, and in the following decades thousands of Caribbean women migrated to Britain to be trained as nurses. Most of them expected to return to practise their profession in their country of origin; however, the vast majority stayed in Britain, and Caribbean nurses have had a strong presence in the British National Health System along with other ethnic and/or racial minorities from Ireland, Africa and Asia. In my recent study of this migration, many of the interviewed nurses chose to emphasise the positive aspects of their British training and career, even though immigrant student nurses often faced racism and structural discrimination. Such problems included being channelled into the shorter training programme for practical nurses, even when they were qualified for the 3-year programme training for registered nurses, being placed in low-prestige wards, such as geriatrics or psychiatry, and assigned to perform the least pleasant duties in the hospital, both during and after completion of their training (Ali 2001, 81; Baxter 1988; Cortis and Rinomhota 1996; Hardill and Macdonald 2000; Dyer, McDowell, and Batnitzky 2008; Batnitzky and McDowell 2011). In this article, I will analyse the nurses' positive perceptions of their British training in terms of the ideological importance of education as an avenue of social and personal mobility in British West Indian society,[1] which had its own social and racial hierarchies, and the social and personal opportunities that became available to the women through their training in the profession of nursing at British hospitals.

The study[2] is based on life-story interviews with 35 female nurses, contacted through the 'snowball' method, who got trained at British hospitals from the 1950s to the 1970s. They originated in ten different Caribbean societies and their educational qualifications ranged from the school-leaving certificate obtained after 7 years of primary school to the senior Cambridge exam taken after secondary school.[3] In the interviews they were encouraged to describe their Caribbean background, the circumstances behind their migration, their training in nursing and the lives this had enabled. The nurses clearly were not oblivious to the problems the immigrants met at the British hospitals in the post-WWII period. Less than a third had been admitted directly into the 3-year course in general nursing, most being accepted initially into shorter courses in practical, mental or fever nursing. They were thus trained in less desirable programmes. Nevertheless, they did not highlight these aspects of their nursing experiences. Rather, they emphasised their determination to not allow discriminatory practices to get in the way of their educational ambitions and described how they succeeded at reaching their goals. They also pointed to the positive experiences of living in a different society and enjoying a new form of freedom with their peers that changed them as persons. This points to the importance of foregrounding the nurses' subject position as young, ambitious migrants pursuing opportunities for social and personal mobility abroad, when investigating this form of educational migration.[4] This analysis will therefore examine how the nurses' experiences were shaped by their subjectivities, understood as 'ensemble[s] of modes of perception, affect, thought, desire, fear, and so forth that animate acting subjects' (Ortner 2005, 31), as well as by the broader historical and societal context in which they were embedded as actors (see Ortner 2005, 46).

In the following, I first address the role of education as a mode of socio-economic mobility in colonial British West Indian societies, emphasising especially the emergence of educated professionals and the role of British education in this development. This leads to a discussion of the nurses' subject position as young migrants, focusing on how the dominance of the British colonial educational system shaped their perceptions of the opportunities offered by training in Britain. Finally, I suggest how this case may further our understanding of this – and other forms of – educational migration.

Education in the Caribbean

By the middle of the twentieth century, the British West Indian societies had undergone a long period of decline, as the formerly so lucrative plantation economy became increasingly unprofitable and the British mother country lost interest in the colonies. When Britain began to recruit workers abroad after the Second World War to meet an acute demand for labour power, West Indians eagerly migrated to seek employment in the factories, the transport sector and the newly established National Health Care System. By the early 1970s, more than half a million West Indians had migrated to Britain (Chamberlain 1998, 6). The number of people who migrated to be trained at the hospitals is small compared to the massive population movement of largely labour migrants and their families, even if it was in the tens of thousands. Indeed, some studies have suggested that the British hospitals treated the young West Indians primarily as an inexpensive source of labour, who needed training in only the most basic nursing skills (Ali 2001, 6; Baxter 1988). The West Indian women, however, saw themselves as youths seeking qualifications within the profession of nursing, spurred by the high value placed on education as an avenue of social and economic mobility within the hierarchical West Indian societies where social class and colour had been closely associated. The significance of education – and the profession of nursing – thus must be seen in the historical context of not just mainland Britain, but also the colonial heritage of the British West Indies.

Race was the foundation of social differentiation in the Caribbean slave societies and by the end of slavery in the mid-1800s, an intricate system of colour distinctions had developed with black slaves in the bottom, mixed-race free coloured in the middle and privileged whites on the top. With the abolishment of slavery, however, race lost official legitimacy as the basis of social stratification. To a great extent, it was replaced by an ideology of education that (re)established class differences 'but without reference to color' (Austin 1983, 236). Education, states Kuper in his study of Jamaica (1976, 74–75), became 'a functional alternative to "race" in the ideological justification of Jamaican social inequality' that is better suited to modern societies. Thus, it 'presents itself as open to achievement, and as a channel for social mobility', but in reality it is 'normally the consequence, not the cause, of high social position'. The colour scale thus remained an important, if often unspoken, mark of class.

A key aspect of education as an ideology legitimising social inequality was the construction of what Levinson and Holland (1996) have termed the 'educated person'. In the West Indies such an 'educated person' was a 'cultured' individual who possessed knowledge of European history, geography and culture and who mastered social skills, such as the ability to speak 'proper' English and display 'good' British manners in the form of gentlemanly behaviour by men, modesty and virtuousness on the part of women. Through the focus on this 'culture of respectability' (Olwig 1993), the West Indian schools thus became important 'sites for the formation of subjectivities through the production and consumption of cultural forms' (Levinson and Holland 1996, 13–14). This subject formation was key to the development of a professional class.

The close link between educational attainment and social mobility was apparent in the occupational opportunities available to the youths. The school-leaving exam offered after 7 years of education in the primary schools opened up for student teaching in the primary schools, whereas a secondary school certificate qualified for teaching at a more advanced level and employment in public service. The opportunities were limited, however. While primary schools were free and accessible in the local communities, secondary schools were few, costly and far between in most British West Indian societies. A few local colleges offered teacher's training, however higher education required further studies at a university abroad.[5] It was therefore restricted to the children (sons) of well-to-do white plantation owners and merchants as well as the handful of students, who did so well on the Cambridge exams that they obtained one of the few island scholarships awarded by the local governments from the latter part of the nineteenth century (Gordon 1963, 240). These scholarships were almost invariably used to study medicine or law, professions that would secure a comfortable livelihood and high social status in the colonial society. The significance of further education as the highest mark of social mobility was reflected in the intense local interest in the youths' scramble for further education. In his memoires, William Besson, recipient of Trinidad's single island scholarship in 1919, thus recalled how people 'followed the success of students as nowadays they follow success in the Derby' (Besson 1989, 41).

The high prestige of medicine and law must be seen in the light of their special status as professions. Professions, according to Evetts (2003, 397), 'are essentially the knowledge-based category of occupations which usually follow a period of tertiary education and vocational training and experience'. This advanced education, Hughes (1963, 656) writes, allows professionals to 'claim, the exclusive right to practise, as a vocation, the arts which they profess to know, and to give the kind of advice derived from their special lines of knowledge'. The notion of a profession thus includes an ideology concerning the need to safeguard the knowledge and skills basic to practising a particular occupation, thereby presumably securing a higher quality of service for the benefit of society, while also requiring a system of control excluding those not deemed qualified to practise the profession. The professionalisation of certain occupations thus went hand in hand with the establishment of a formalised educational system as a legitimate mode of social stratification. Only those with official documentation proving possession of the knowledge and skills required to perform a particular occupation would be allowed to practise the profession.

The nursing profession

Unlike the other professions that became established in the West Indies during the post-emancipation period, nursing has had a long history in the West Indies linked to the social mobility of black women. During slavery, the plantation societies relied to a great extent on the services of African–Caribbean women for the care of the black as well as the white population (De Barros, Palmer, and Wright 2009, 1). While these women worked formally under white officials, they drew primarily on African traditions of herbal medicine and practised quite independently. They, therefore, had a position of respect and privilege in the local communities. Nursing, combined with healing, was also an important occupation for free-coloured women who often lived in the towns. A prominent example was the 'doctress' Mary Seacole, a Jamaican free coloured born in 1805 who 'came from a long line of Creole women trained in the herbal arts' but who had also learned some medicinal skills from European doctors treating European guests at her lodging house (Hewitt 2002, 5–6; see also Seacole 2005[1857]; Salih 2005). She earned quite a reputation for her good 'care of sick British army and naval officers and their wives' (Rappaport 2005, 9).[6]

After the slaves' 1834 emancipation in the British West Indies, an increasing concern for the general population's health led to the development of a more formal system of treatment based on Western medicine. General hospitals were erected, medical doctors trained abroad were hired and trained British nurses were recruited to teach modern nursing to the local care-giving staff at the hospitals. An important aspect of the nurses' mission was to 'counteract negative attributes of the colonial environment by recreating the more civilised standards of medical care available at home' (Howell, Rafferty, and Snaith 2011, 1158). Their success was limited, judging from a commission investigating social and economic conditions in the British West Indies during the 1930s, because it severely criticised the local health systems and called for a formal training programme for nurses (Hewitt 2002, 7). During the 1930s, Nurses Associations began to be established mainly by local nurses trained abroad, and acts were introduced to regulate the practice and training of midwives and nurses. It was not before the early 1950s, however, that formal training programmes in nursing were instituted at the main hospitals (Hewitt 2002; Hunte 2009, 311–322).

During the early 1950s, when the migration of student nurses to Britain began, nursing had a somewhat ambiguous position in the British West Indies. On the one hand, it was a centuries-old, highly respected occupation for African–Caribbean women of key importance in the local communities; on the other hand, those seeking to professionalise the health sector regarded it with suspicion. One of the nurses interviewed recalled:

> My great grandmother was a midwife, and she delivered babies in Barbados. [...] My father thought that the doctors did not like her, because they felt somewhat threatened by her, but still they depended on her skills and the good work that she did. I followed her sometimes and saw how she would pick various herbs that she would tell the mothers to use for healing drinks. So she was more than a midwife, she was more generally into healing [...] When she died, there was a huge funeral attended by a large number of people, because those she had delivered as babies and the mothers she had assisted came.

The description indicates that the medical doctors resented the African–Caribbean healers' encroachment on their profession, yet were not able to manage without them. The healers were losing ground, however, as formal training at the hospitals and possession of an official licence became required by the mid-1900s. At the same time, this formalising of nursing meant that it was becoming a desirable profession conferring a position of respectability in the colonial society.

The ability to obtain qualifications in a respectable profession was the main reason mentioned by the nurses for training in Britain. One of them stated: 'If you were a nurse, you know, you were looked up to by people. [...] It was very much a "badge of honor"!' The professional status of nurses was signalled by their official uniform and several remembered a prominent attraction of nursing being the 'crisp white uniform' they had seen the 'top nurses' wear at West Indian hospitals. Many also emphasised being attracted to nursing because they liked to care for others. They wanted to do so in a professional capacity, however, not as overburdened mothers. As one nurse noted: 'I always said, "I must have a profession before I ever marry" [...] because my mother had all these children, I might end up the same way'.

If nursing had emerged as an attractive profession by the mid-1900s, the West Indian training programmes were still in their infancy and generally not as highly regarded as the British programmes (Hunte 2009, 328–337). Furthermore, they could only accommodate a fraction of the many young women eager to become nurses, and were widely believed to select students on the basis of personal connections rather than personal qualifications. 'It is not what you know, but who you know', several explained; the further down the social and colour scale one was, the fewer powerful personal connections, and opportunities, one likely would have. When the British hospitals began recruiting student nurses in the West Indies, thereby offering what in the British colonies was believed to be the best quality training, thousands of young women migrated to Britain. Many were strongly encouraged by their parents who saw a good future in the profession. One mother, a successful seamstress, made it clear: 'Nursing is a vocation, it's a career. Seamstress is not'.

As the nurses' narratives show, their migration to train in a profession was driven by a range of different feelings. They saw a great opportunity in the obtainment of professional qualifications in nursing in Britain, but their decision to become nurses was also grounded in their admiration for older relatives practising the age-old African–Caribbean art of nursing; they were proud of their good upbringing and education, but were constrained by the continued favouring of personal connections rather than qualifications; they were keen to pursue professional goals that would increase their own and their family's status in the colonial society, but they also desired a life of their own. In the following, I show how these mixed, even contradictory feelings shaped the early experiences of nursing in Britain.

Training in the British hospitals

The British hospitals of the post-WWII period have been characterised as regimes of 'Victorian authority' where nurses were 'restrained by the discipline which

17

matrons had imposed on them, by their loyalty to their group and to their hospital, and by the spirit of uncomplaining service which was taken to be the heritage of their profession' (Abel-Smith 1977[1960], 245). The hospitals' attempt to maintain a highly disciplined and controlling environment is regarded as a main reason why a nursing career was not attractive to women in post-war British society, where gender roles were rapidly changing (Dingwall, Rafferty, and Webster 1988, 119). The Caribbean nurses, however, were very positive about the training they received. Indeed, they seem to have viewed the strict discipline and demanding work routines as an integral part of the high quality training they received:

> I remember my tutor now, she was tough, she was *tough*, but had real standards. [...] Many of us, we were like kids, we had never left home, but none of that whimpering, and what have you, you were supposed to be there at 8 o'clock: *'I want you here at 8 o'clock'*. And you had to set up your trolley, and everything had to be absolutely *perfect* on these trolleys. [...] We saw it as tough. But in fact we appreciated her very much for that. It was very, very good. [Emphasis in original.]

Another nurse described the matrons and sisters as 'stern' but concerned that the student nurses 'did everything right' and 'were well-trained':

> You had to learn how to clean floors, how to clean lockers, do the flowers. You had to learn the hygiene of patients   do their teeth, bed baths   you know, this is all strict   how to make beds, everything like that, very much, you know, regulated.

The nurses generally do not seem to have minded the hospitals' hierarchical structure as such, being used to respecting authority in the equally Victorian West Indies, whether in the family, school or church: 'They were very strict, but [...] it didn't infringe on me, because I was coming from a society that was very strict anyway'. Another nurse stated matter-of-factly that she never questioned the way the hospitals were run:

> You just did it, because that is what you were there for, to learn and so, yeah. Okay, they had one or two people who had a rebellious streak but most, the large majority of people, just did the job and they enjoyed it.

The student nurses also generally went along with the strict rules of the nurses' home where they resided during their training. This meant living under the watchful eyes of a senior resident nurse, having no visitors in the rooms and being back at a set time in the evening.

The hospital environment, with its authoritarian structure, where the senior staff was to be respected and obeyed, and with its concern to safeguard the respectability of young ladies, validated the social norms and cultural values the student nurses had grown up with in the Caribbean. Indeed, some of the nurses felt superior to the local British population that did not always abide by such norms:

> I must say I was disappointed about certain standards; especially the food and the way people conducted themselves and so on. Because we came from a very strict background and I was just a little bit surprised at how people behaved.

This feeling of belonging to a better class of people gave the nurses some immunity against the racism that they met in the hospitals. Many, thus, dismissed racist patients as people of the lower segment of society, who were characterised by poor upbringing and ignorance. One nurse, for example, recalled her reaction when a patient complimented her on her ability to walk in shoes and speak English, thinking that she came from some far-away, primitive place:

> I thought to myself, I could be very rude to this woman, but I looked at her age and decided, it's not nice. 'I am going to tell you something', I said, 'where I come from there is only one language and that is the English language. [...] I think that I speak this language so much better than you, all of you, and even the queen'.

The women's acceptance of the hospital hierarchy, and the authoritarian system that went along with it, did not necessarily mean that they endorsed this hierarchy. Rather, it reflected their pragmatic realisation that this was necessary to become a nurse. As one person explained, 'I'm the sort of person that just forgets things and just moves on. My whole intention was to train, reach as far as I can ... and that's it'. As long as they were treated on par with the other student nurses and managed to make their way through the system, they were therefore rather accommodating. Behind this appearance of compliance, however, many engaged in various acts of small-scale resistance. Several thought, for example, that the matrons had been obsessed with keeping a clean and orderly hospital and less concerned with looking after, and talking with, the patients. They, therefore, developed their own routines with the patients, but made sure to be busy with acceptable nursing tasks whenever the matron appeared on the ward. Apparently, some patients were aware of this double play and warned the nurses when the matron was coming. Furthermore, several nurses recalled having returned late to the nurses' home and jumping over the fence or bribing the guard to open the gate. Direct confrontations were more rare and less successful. The nurse, who hemmed up her uniform because she liked to wear short skirts, was quickly pulled aside by the matron and made to wear a 'proper' uniform.

While the student nurses were willing to accept hierarchical structures based on seniority and formal qualifications, they were less accepting of systems of discrimination that impeded their progress or resulted in unfair treatment. This was most strongly expressed in relation to the obstacles against doing the general nursing programmes for state registered nurses (SRN). As noted, only about a third of the women interviewed began their nursing career in the SRN programme. The others were initially placed in programmes for mental, fever[7] or practical nursing (SEN) that were regarded as less attractive. About half of them explained that they were trained in these programmes because they lacked the educational qualifications for the SRN programme.[8] The other half said they had the qualifications for the SRN programme, but did not realise the limitations of the training programme for which they were admitted. This was a fate they shared with many other overseas students and which has been attributed to racism (see Cortis and Rinomhota 1996, 360; Hardill and Macdonald 2000, 684).

The women reacted in different ways to this discrimination. One nursing student simply quit the SEN programme after 3 months, deciding it was a waste of her time since she would not receive the qualifications she wanted. Furthermore, she was dissatisfied with the way she was treated by a ward sister who, she thought, had scolded her unfairly and behaved in a disrespectful manner. With her educational qualifications, she quickly became accepted for the SRN programme at another hospital. Several other nurses, who found themselves in the training programme for practical nurses, upgraded their qualifications immediately after finishing their initial training. Some SEN trained, however, were not able to upgrade before the 1990s, when conversion courses were offered.[9] They, therefore, had to continue with the physically demanding care work, or they essentially performed the tasks of SRN nurses but without getting the status, recognition or pay that went along with it. While they described facing many difficulties, their primary message was not the suffering and discrimination they had endured, but rather the willpower and dedication that enabled them to obtain full qualifications:

> I worked really hard; my daughter was little, my husband worked shift and of course I was studying and working shift as well. So it was quite, quite difficult from my personal point of view, but I was determined so we did our exams one year later. [...] An Asian girl and I passed with distinction.

Peer relations

At the same time as the nurses were incorporated into the hierarchical, authoritarian hospital regime, they developed relations of a completely different nature with peers. Thus, they emphasised how fellow student nurses supported each other in their work and studies, kept each other company in the nurses' home and went out together in their free time. Many were at hospitals with large groups of student nurses from the Caribbean and were therefore able to (re)create a Caribbean form of sociality with each other. One nurse remembered with envy how Caribbean friends at other hospitals got together as a group and enjoyed 'cooking their own food, straightening their hair, things like that, playing music' – something that was impossible at the prestigious University College Hospital in London, where she trained as the only black person. The nurses also recalled friendships with Irish student nurses, who, like the Caribbean students, were recruited to meet the shortage of care workers at the British hospitals and often placed in the shorter 2-year programmes.[10] They would go out together to concerts, dance halls or to local pubs: 'We were young, we were girls of the same age, and we had fun, you know. We used to go out in the evening to the pub – the Irish girls, they liked the pub – and we used to make a fool out of ourselves!'

The nurses described the possibility of going out on their own after work as a form of independence they never knew in the Caribbean. As one noted: 'I remember the first time I realised, I don't really have to ask anybody for permission, I can just do my own thing!' Another nurse recalled the elation she felt when she realised freedom she enjoyed in England, but also the heavy responsibility that came with this freedom:

> I felt I was my own individual […]. I can now make decisions […]. But at the end of it, I knew that I had to make everything right. I had to make sure that whatever decisions I made there were some good outcomes, because I couldn't afford to fail. Because if you fail, what do you do? You [   ] don't return with nothing. You had to return having made something of your life.

A few did not manage to 'make everything right', but spent too much time partying, getting involved with guys or just watching television instead of studying with the result that they failed exams. They eventually completed their training, but remembered fellow student nurses who never finished. The ability to enjoy the freedom gained, while keeping up with the training, therefore was an important skill that had to be mastered.

The sociality that they experienced with their peers broke in several ways with the social norms they knew from the Caribbean. It not only gave them a new sense of personal freedom, it also exposed them to social milieus, such as bars, clubs and dance halls that they could not have frequented in the Caribbean, and it brought them into contact with youths of varying social and cultural background. One woman from St. Lucia, whose parents had prohibited her from learning the French Creole spoken by the lower class on the island, described, for example, how she learned the language from Haitians she met at a dance hall. This opened up for socialising with a broad segment of St. Lucians in London, because they liked to speak the French Creole at their parties.

Through their peer relations, the student nurses furthermore made friends with people from other Caribbean islands as well as different Commonwealth countries and Britain, whether fellow student nurses or people met outside the hospital. They, therefore, gradually developed a new form of belonging grounded in their shared Caribbean origins, their common background of having immigrated from the British Commonwealth, and their partaking in the modern youth culture in Britain. As one nurse stated, 'that was the beginning of my independence, living away from home and associating with people from all over the world so to speak'. This independence is reflected in the nurses' choices of partners, which included persons from different Caribbean societies, other British Commonwealth areas and Britain as well as their Caribbean place of origin.

Accounts of the social life with peers inside and outside the hospital, as well as the personal freedom experienced in the British society, loomed large in the nurses' narratives. Indeed, when asked to describe their training in Britain, the nurses often talked about these dimensions of their stay at the hospitals, rather than the actual teaching, supervision and experience they received in the nursing profession.

Practising the profession

The young women generally planned to spend only as much time in Britain as was necessary to receive their qualifications in nursing and midwifery, and then return to the Caribbean to enjoy a good career in the profession. One of the nurses explained:

> [Training in England] was the best in nursing. That was the expectation. So my expectation was, if I trained in nursing in England, I might go back as a qualified nurse, and eventually work up the ladder, because my expectation was to go back. And I wanted to be a matron.

She did not move back as anticipated, neither did the large majority of the Caribbean nurses who trained in Britain. One reason for this lack of return migration, as some authors have suggested (Ali 2001; Baxter 1988), is that those who had received qualifications in practical nursing were not entitled to practise the profession of nursing in the Caribbean. They would therefore be forced to do unskilled work at the hospitals, for example as ward assistants (Hunte 2009, 93), that did not match their actual qualifications. Nor did it agree with their ambition to return as respected members of the nursing profession and they therefore preferred to remain in Britain where they would be regarded as nurses, even if they worked under certain restrictions.

This problem, however, did not figure as a major issue in the nurses' life stories. The main reason they gave for not moving back was that they cherished the 'freedom' they had acquired in Britain and were not willing to subject themselves again to the authority of the elders in the Caribbean family. As one (SEN-trained) nurse said when explaining why she had stayed in Britain, 'I had got used to having my own things, and doing my own thing, and as much as you wanted to be with your family then, over 2 years I'd forged that out for myself really, you know, so I suppose it was the natural thing to do'. As part of this forging a life out for themselves, many of the women were marrying and settling down in Britain with their own families. This, of course, complicated return migration, especially if spouses were not from the same Caribbean society or had not both acquired formal qualifications entitling them to a good job upon their return. While the young nurses by and large opted to stay in Britain, most made a point of visiting their family in the Caribbean after they had acquired their qualifications. They described being treated as 'royalty' in the home community and sometimes the proud family would put a notice in the paper describing their accomplishments in Britain. By staying in Britain, yet maintaining close ties to family in the Caribbean, they therefore continued to enjoy the social and the personal mobility associated with their professional training.

Several nurses did return to the Caribbean later in their careers, after having established their own families, because they wished to help build up the newly independent Caribbean countries.[11] The nurses who returned in this way, however, often experienced difficulty practising their profession. They found that the locally trained nurses did not display the same discipline and professionalism that they knew from the British system and showed little interest in learning anything from their British-trained colleagues. These women therefore gave up having a career in the Caribbean and moved back to Britain with their family.[12] By returning to Britain, they not only abandoned their original plans to practise nursing in the Caribbean, but actively chose to live in Britain, having realised that they enjoyed the life they had created there and that they were pleased with their British nursing career. As one nurse concluded, 'I have done well in nursing in spite of the fact I didn't break the glass ceiling. I went as far as I wanted to go. [...] Okay, there probably have been times when things haven't looked so attractive but generally I can genuinely say that I have enjoyed my nursing career'.

Conclusion

This article has explored how Caribbean nurses' educational experiences in post-WWII Britain were shaped by their subject positions as young women from highly stratified late-colonial societies where training in a profession had key ideological importance as an avenue of social mobility. The nurses' life stories show that both their migration for training in the profession of nursing and their decision to make their career in Britain were shaped by ambiguous, even contra-dictory, feelings. These included the desire to carry on time-honoured family traditions of African–Caribbean nursing, but within the framework of a modern nursing profession based on formal training; yearning for the social recognition associated with the profession of nursing, yet disappointment at the opportunities offered in the Caribbean; ambitions to live up to parents' educational expecta-tions and fears of returning with nothing, yet insistence on maintaining the personal freedom gained abroad. These many different feelings reflect the nurses' complex subject position as individuals who were proud of their achievements in the nursing profession, yet at the same time reflected critically upon the particular set of circumstances in which they found themselves (cf. Ortner 2005, 45). In these reflections, they were not only concerned with the formal training they received in the nursing profession at the British hospitals. They also considered the conditions in their country of origin that compelled them to leave for further education; the friendships with peers and the freedom to engage in a new life abroad that they enjoyed, and their situation as educated professionals gauging their options in the Caribbean and Britain. Finally, the nurses' narratives were influenced by their position as mature adults reconsidering the choices they had made throughout their life. Educational migration and mobility thus are linked through subjective experiences that are shaped by, and in turn shape, the social, cultural and personal contexts of individual migrants' lives. When examining migration for educational purposes, and the mobility it may enable, it is therefore important to be mindful of not only the official qualifications that may have been obtained, and the formal career paths they enabled, but also the wider conditions of life that may make such migration a favoured option. The analysis thus points to the importance of applying a temporal perspective that includes both the broader historical context of migration for educational purposes and the more personal life perspectives of the individual migrants who seek to benefit from it.

Notes

1. The terms 'West Indian' and 'Caribbean' can be used interchangeably, but 'West Indian' is used here mainly to refer to the British colonies and their subjects.
2. The interviewed nurses' help is gratefully acknowledged as is economic support from Aksel Tovborg Jensens Legat, the University of Copenhagen and the Carlsberg Foundation. I have benefited from comments on earlier versions of the paper presented at London South Bank University, University of Oxford, Australian Association for Caribbean Studies, National Institute of Advanced Studies in Bangalore, St. Andrews University, University of Sussex, Aarhus University and San Diego State University.
3. Two nurses of Caribbean background born in Britain as well as three male nurses and two female care assistants born in the Caribbean were also interviewed. Limitations of space prevent an analysis of these interviews, and the light they can shed on issues of gender and class within the nursing profession.
4. For another study emphasising the nurses' agency, see Flynn's (2011) monograph on West Indian nurses who migrated to Canada upon completion of their British training.
5. This changed when the University of the West Indies was established in 1948.
6. Seacole travelled to Britain and, like Florence Nightingale, cared for British soldiers in the Crimean War. She never achieved the social recognition Nightingale enjoyed in British society (Rappaport 2005; Salih 2005).
7. Fever hospitals treated patients with high fever caused by various illnesses. When they closed during the 1960s, the fever nurses had to retrain.
8. When the qualifications were formalised in 1962, SRN training required five O levels, SEN training two O levels (Webb 2000, 116).
9. All the interviewed SEN trained nurses, except for one who became ill, eventually upgraded their training.
10. For a study of Irish nurses, who trained in the post WWII period, see Ryan (2007).
11. Some responded to a call by their Caribbean country of origin for educated nationals to return.
12. Some nurses did stay. An analysis of their situation is beyond the scope of this paper.

References

Abel Smith, B. 1977[1960]. *A History of the Nursing Profession*. London: Heinemann.

Ali, L. 2001. "West Indian Nurses and the National Health Service in Britain 1950 1968." MA diss., University of York.

Austin, D. J. 1983. "Culture and Ideology in the English Speaking Caribbean: A View from Jamaica." *American Ethnologist* 10 (2): 223 240. doi:10.1525/ae.1983.10.2.02a00010.

Batnitzky, A., and L. McDowell. 2011. "Migration, Nursing, Institutional Discrimination and Emotional/Affective Labour: Ethnicity and Labour Stratification in the UK National Health Service." *Social & Cultural Geography* 12 (2): 181 201. doi:10.1080/14649365.2011.545142.

Baxter, C. 1988. *The Black Nurse: An Endangered Species*. Cambridge: National Extension College.

Besson, J., ed. 1989. *Caribbean Reflections: The Life and Times of a Trinidad Scholar (1901 1986). An Oral History Narrated by William W. Besson*. London: Karia Press.

Chamberlain, M. 1998. "Introduction." In *Caribbean Migration. Globalised Identitites*, edited by M. Chamberlain, 1 17. London: Routledge.

Cortis, J. D., and A. S. Rinomhota. 1996. "The Future of Ethnic Minority Nurses in the NHS." *Journal of Nursing Management* 4 (6): 359 366. doi:10.1111/j.1365 2834.1996.tb00007.x.

De Barros, J., S. Palmer, and D. Wright. 2009. "Introduction." In *Health and Medicine in the Circum Caribbean, 1800 1968*, edited by J. De Barros, S. Palmer, and D. Wright, 1 18. New York, NY: Routledge.

Dingwall, R., A. M. Rafferty, and C. Webster. 1988. *An Introduction to the Social History of Nursing*. London: Routledge.

Dyer, S., L. McDowell, and A. Batnitzky. 2008. "Emotional Labour/Body Work: The Caring Labours of Migrants in the UK's National Health Service." *Geoforum* 39: 2030 2038. doi:10.1016/j.geoforum.2008.08.005.

Evetts, J. 2003. "The Sociological Analysis of Professionalism: Occupational Change in the Modern World." *International Sociology* 18 (2): 395 415. doi:10.1177/ 0268580903018002005.

Flynn, K. 2011. *Moving beyond Borders. A History of Black Canadian and Caribbean Women in Diapora*. Toronto: University of Toronto Press.

Gordon, S. 1963. *A Century of West Indian Education*. London: Longmans.

Hardill, I., and S. Macdonald. 2000. "Skilled International Migration: The Experience of Nurses in the UK." *Regional Studies* 34 (7): 681 692. doi:10.1080/00343400050178465.

Hewitt, H. H. 2002. *Trailblazers in Nursing Education: A Caribbean Perspective, 1946 1986*. Kingston: Canoe Press.

Howell, J., A. M. Rafferty, and A. Snaith. 2011. "(Author)ity Abroad: The Life Writing of Colonial Nurses." *International Journal of Nursing Studies* 48 (9): 1155 1162. doi:10.1016/j.ijnurstu.2011.03.010.

Hughes, E. C. 1963. "Professions." *Daedalus* 92 (4): 655 668.

Hunte, E. I. 2009. *The Unsung Nightingales. The Development of Nursing in Barbados 1844 2000*. Barbados: E.I. Hunte.

Kuper, A. 1976. *Changing Jamaica*. London: Routledge & Kegan Paul.

Levinson, B. A., and D. Holland. 1996. "The Cultural Production of the Educated Person: An Introduction." In *The Cultural Production of the Educated Person. Critical Ethnographies of Schooling and Local Practice*, edited by B. A. Levinson, D. E. Foley, and D. Holland, 1 54. Albany: State University of New York Press.

Olwig, K. F. 1993. *Global Culture, Island Identity: Continuity and Change in the Afro Caribbean Community of Nevis*. Reading, MA: Harwood.

Ortner, S. B. 2005. "Subjectivity and Cultural Critique." *Anthropological Theory* 5 (1): 31 52. doi:10.1177/1463499605050867.

Rappaport, H. 2005. "The Invitation that Never Came. Mary Seacole after the Crimea." *History Today* 55 (2): 9 15.

Ryan, L. 2007. "Who Do You Think You Are? Irish Nurses Encountering Ethnicity and Constructing Identity in Britain." *Ethnic and Racial Studies* 30 (3): 416 438. doi:10.1080/01419870701217498.

Salih, S. 2005. "Introduction." In *Wonderful Adventures of Mrs. Seacole in Many Lands by Mary Seacole*, edited by S. Salih, xv lii. London: Penguin.

Seacole, M. 2005[1857]. *Wonderful Adventures of Mrs. Seacole in Many Lands*. Edited by S. Salih. London: Penguin.

Webb, B. 2000. "Enrolled Nurse Conversion: A Review of the Literature." *Journal of Nursing Management* 8 (2): 115 120. doi:10.1046/j.1365 2834.2000.00153.x.

Rescuing children, reforming the Empire: British child migration to colonial Southern Rhodesia

Katja Uusihakala

This article examines a child migration scheme which aimed at permanently resettling British children to Southern Rhodesia during 1946 1962. First, the philanthropic scheme was framed in terms of child welfare; it sought to benefit selected children by removing them from their homes and resettling them at Rhodesia Fairbridge Memorial College, a boarding school and children's home. Second, the scheme aimed at advancing Empire building more broadly by increasing the number of white citizens in Africa. The article considers how the Fairbridge scheme distinctively combined physical and social mobility. The children were expected, through first class educa tion, to rise to privileged positions, thus maintaining the colonial, racially segregated social hierarchy. By focusing on implicit forms of education at the boarding school, analysed as a 'Goffmanian' total institution, the article considers the ambiguous intents and outcomes of a very particular project of colonial social engineering.

As an Imperial investment the scheme must appeal to everyone who believes in the great mission of the British Commonwealth of Nations, and to every lover of children. (The Rhodesia Fairbridge Memorial College Scheme)

Nice to know we were an investment! Who collected the dividends? Yes we were 'well looked after' per se, but what about the feeling of utter abandonment suffered by many at the time, and then years of coming to terms with 'being different', a ward of the state, when our parents were still alive? We didn't get to choose this path. (A response from the 'Children'; Kingsley Fairbridge Scholars Reunion Webpage 2002)

Introduction

The Rhodesia Fairbridge Memorial College was established on the outskirts of Bulawayo in Southern Rhodesia (Zimbabwe) in a disused Royal Air Force training base in 1946. The school ran until 1962 as a boarding school and a home for British child emigrants, aged 5–13. The goals of the migration scheme were twofold. First, the scheme was framed in terms of child welfare; it sought to benefit underprivileged children 'of solid British stock' by offering them an education in a healthy and wholesome rural setting in a settler colony. Second, it aimed at contributing to the advancement of the Empire more broadly by increasing 'the strength and numerical superiority of the British element in Africa',[1] exemplifying, albeit in a rather extreme form, Britain's post-war migration policies.

The practice of resettling British children in the dominions had originated already in the seventeenth century when orphaned apprentices were sent to the North American territories (Boucher 2009, 914). In the late nineteenth century child migration became something of a mass movement; various charitable societies sought to rescue children from unfortunate situations and to transplant them in the colonies.[2] A novel awareness of the phenomenon was awakened in the 1990s with the publication of a number of child migrant autobiographies and popular histories. The ensuing debate has stressed the perennial pain and trauma that the ripping apart of families and the maltreatment of some of the children has caused to the migrants. The debate culminated in 2010, when Prime Minister Gordon Brown made a public apology to the child migrants on behalf of the nation calling the transportation of 130,000[3] British children to the dominions a 'shameful episode' in British history (BBC News, February 24, 2010).

The ambition of the Rhodesian migration scheme, managed by a voluntary organization, the Fairbridge Society, was to craft the chosen children into ideal colonial citizens. This involved careful selection of the right kind of child migrants and their systematic upbringing in the educational institution. In order to be considered suitable to be educated into managerial positions in a racially segregated colonial society, the children needed to have a sufficiently high IQ, reasonably solid family background and to be of sound physical and mental health. Conversely, the wrong kind of a child was seen susceptible to the proximity of the African majority and thus vulnerable to 'slippage' when it came to upholding racial boundaries.

The mobility of persons, possessions, ideas and practices between home and away has been considered paramount to the formation of imperial identities. In such movements the boundaries of the British domestic sphere and that of the empire appear constantly blurred. In British colonies such as India and Kenya, physical mobility was intrinsically tied to social advancement; upper-class settler families often aspired to send their children back to Britain to be educated. According to Elizabeth Buettner, in colonial India 'a white bourgeois identity became predicated upon travels to, and formal education in, Britain' (2004, 9). Children's boarding school upbringing 'at home' reflected the families' socio-economic standing and confirmed it in the future. Leaving India to be educated in Britain was 'a rite of passage that positioned an individual within the transient, sojourner, better-off community marked as European' (Buettner 2004, 80), whereas the status of those European children who were schooled in India indicated racial ambiguity.

In the case of the Fairbridge College scheme, the emigrant children's movement was to the opposite direction but for a similar end. The children migrated from England to Rhodesia for an education, which was to open a route for social advancement and to create and consolidate the white racial identity of the colony. The aims of both the senders (the parents and the organizing society) and the receivers (the Rhodesian state) were convergent. The parents sought to offer a better chance in life for their children, whereas the Rhodesian state strove, by bringing 'pure blood' into the colony, to reinvigorate the European civilization of the country and thereby to legitimate the endurance of the position and stature of the colony's white population. Thus, although the Fairbridge children were rarely the knowledgeable agents of their own migration, their movement can be seen as part of a much broader frame in which imperial identities were being grounded in mobility.

Mobility then may be considered as a defining feature of imperial identities, its prerequisite as well as its outcome. The Fairbridge scheme reveals, however, that imperial ideas and practices related to physical and social mobility were characterized by contradiction and friction. By examining the intents and outcomes of the scheme, this article aims to bring to light tensions that exist between ideas of mobility and immobility and of freedom and constraint, which delineate the scheme. Whereas the outline sketched a resilient and mobile imperial identity for the children, the colonial state stressed the rooting of the migrants; their mobility was to end in Rhodesia, which the children were to make their permanent home. But although the metropolitan and colonial scheme planners might have differed on the desirable scope of physical mobility, their ambition for the children's social mobility was mutual. Moving from the level of design to the way the scheme was put to practice reveals related tensions. The spatial and temporal arrangements of the Fairbridge College formed a particular amalgamation of constraint and freedom, which reflected the attempt to bring up disciplined and civilized colonial citizens socialized into settler ways of belonging to the land.

In their analysis of child migration, scholars such as Boucher (2014), Harper and Constantine (2010) and Paul (2001) have also emphasized migration to the empire as a means for social advancement. My intention is to add to this scholarship by focusing on how these goals were realized in a boarding school institution the aims and outcomes of which were, in part, totalizing. I consider in particular how the socialization and learning that took place outside the classroom can be seen as instrumental for the production of colonial, racially segregated social structure in which the migrant children were sketched a privileged position. I explore to what extent the Fairbridge College may be considered a 'Goffmanian' total institution, which sought to socialize the children by a strict temporal and spatial design. Like boarding schools generally, the College controlled the children's schedules and constrained their daily movements – but only to a certain degree. In order to bring up the children as proper settler citizens, the timetable allowed for considerable freedom of movement in the surrounding countryside. I will argue that this tension of constraint and freedom becomes essential in understanding the particular kinds of imperial identities that were being created in this scheme.

This article is based on ongoing research[4]; archival material has been collected in the United Kingdom, and these data are complemented by interviews conducted in South Africa and the United Kingdom. So far interviews have been carried out with 10 people on several occasions. In addition to recorded discussions I have communicated with eight other former Fairbridgians by e-mail. The informants have provided me with materials such as letters, photographs and autobiographical texts. I also draw on published biographical material, most importantly a collection of autobiographies by 24 former Fairbridgians (Windows 2001). Because the records on the Rhodesia Fairbridge scheme are scant, the research will be grounded mostly on personal memories of the alumni, their divergent reflections on the experience of migration and their lives at the College.

The Fairbridge Memorial College scheme in Rhodesia

The Rhodesia Fairbridge Memorial College was founded in the honour of Kingsley Fairbridge, a South African-born social reformer raised on a settler farm in Southern Rhodesia. Fairbridge had long dreamt of populating the 'unpopulated and uncultivated' African spaces with young Britons living in crowded, unhealthy cities (Sherington and Jeffery 1998, 5–6). This vision was strengthened as he became a Rhodes Scholar at Oxford in 1908. The following year Fairbridge, together with fellow students, established a child emigration society, which later became the Fairbridge Society. In addition to rescuing neglected children from urban squalor, Fairbridge reasoned, child emigration would shield and sustain the British identity of the settler empire (Boucher 2009, 922). He sought to achieve these socially and imperially beneficial goals by establishing farm schools, which would train British migrant children in agricultural and domestic skills. According to Boucher, the emphasis on moral coaching was pivotal in Fairbridge's vision; the aspiration was to 'remake the children's bodies, minds and spirits (...) and to create independent and skillful imperial farmers' (Boucher 2009). As such, Fairbridge's project materialized in Australia and not in Africa, since Rhodesia of the early twentieth century was thought by the British government authorities to be too primitive for child migration.[5]

In the late 1930s, the Fairbridge Society began outlining a new kind of a child emigration scheme located in Rhodesia. This scheme differed markedly from the society's previous projects. Whereas in Australia, the children were trained as skilled farm and domestic workers, the child migrants in Rhodesia were to aim for the higher professions and elite positions. 'The difference symbolizes the essential difference between Australia and Southern Rhodesia,' a publicity brochure explains, 'in Australia all work is done by White men; in Southern Rhodesia, all unskilled and a good deal of the semi-skilled work is done by non-Europeans. The Whites, to hold their own, must be well-educated, trained and efficient.'[6]

The founding of the Fairbridge College was not only in the interest of British child rescuers or imperial settlement promoters; the scheme had influential supporters in the colony as well. While the scheme was administered by a London-based Council and travel costs and maintenance partly funded by the UK government, the Rhodesian government bore the greatest responsibility by supplying the premises for the College and providing free education and boarding for the children. Sir Godfrey Huggins, the prime minister of Rhodesia from 1933 until 1953, was strongly in favour of the college. Southern Rhodesia, Huggins pointed out, was a country where there were 'comparatively speaking a handful of white people (...) and a large number of negroes.'[7] To level out this perceived imbalance of population[8] and to counter the threat that upwardly mobile Africans were seen to pose on the legitimation of the privileged position of the whites, Huggins considered the Fairbridge College to be a 'very necessary adjunct to the birth rate.'[9]

The education of European children had long been regarded as a politically pivotal question in the colony, a key factor in maintaining the superior racial status of the whites. The whites feared competition from educated Africans, although the allocation of state aid to European education remained disproportionate compared to African education (Summers 1994, 248–251). The white community itself was felt to be threatened by degeneration and loss of civilization; it was feared that poor whites (often implicitly Afrikaners) would compromise standards of Europeanness (Lowry 2010, 124). This threat was battled by attempts to wipe out social inequalities within the colony's European population – mainly British and Afrikaner – and strengthen the racial solidarity of whites through education.

The educational ambition was to form a new Rhodesian identity which appeared, however, predominately British. English was used as the medium of instruction in government schools, the teaching of Empire history and geography was emphasized in the curriculum, the Union Jack was flown and the British national anthem sung at schools as a matter of course. When recruiting teachers, R. J. Challis writes (1982, 55), preference was given to teachers with boarding school experience and an interest in extra-curricular activities, such as rugby, football, cricket and cadet work (military training) or scouting. It was likely that such teachers would be produced by English public schools. In discussions concerning the reform of white educational policy in the late 1930s, it was underlined that only through 'the very best education' would the whites be able 'to hold their own.' Huggins voiced the concern emphatically: 'Although our youth may be able to play Rugby football and to preserve their white skins with rifles and differential legislation, they will not be able to preserve the white brain, and if they are to survive it will be by nothing except by superior education and intelligence.'[10] Such debates over education and civilization – and the extent to which the maintenance of racial standards were seen to require protection and political effort – reveal, as Ann Laura Stoler (1989) and others (e.g. Kennedy 1987; Mlambo 2000) have demonstrated, how intricately entwined the colonial construction of whiteness was with that of class.

The Second World War suspended the launching of the Fairbridge scheme, and the College finally opened in 1946 with the first batch of 18 boys arriving in December. The first girls arrived in 1948, but boys remained a clear majority of the migrants. Compared to the number of children sent to Australian and Canadian Fairbridge institutions, the Rhodesian scheme was small scale; between 1946 and 1962 altogether 276 British children were sent to Rhodesia. These migrants remained wards of the state until the age of 21, and the warden of the College was responsible for finding the students their first employment after finishing school. The first jobs ranged from farming apprenticeships to banking, from sales jobs to civil service positions. Some continued their studies at university. The varied career paths that followed correspond closely to those of other white urban Rhodesians at the time. According to written autobiographies, where a genre-typical stress on upward movement is often pronounced, most Fairbridgians appear to have done well in their lives, and many have ended up in managerial positions in the civil service or private sector.

Selecting the right kind of child

I have traced some key debates in the Rhodesian educational policies prior to the establishment of the College in order to outline the social and political concerns, which motivated the foundation of the migration scheme. Such concerns were particularly conspicuous in the process of selecting suitable children. For the scheme to benefit Rhodesia, it was essential that the children were 'of the right kind'; of the kind that would be able to 'preserve the white brain' and thus to help keep the higher ranks of the society white. It was also felt that mere intelligence would not sufficiently guarantee that the children would cope in the social and political position into which they were placed. A committee report brings forward such considerations:

> If early life is spent in psychologically and morally disturbed and distressing conditions, the subject becomes liable to develop a petty minded and aggressive attitude of dominance towards a subordinate, which in this particular instance would be a native. Therefore, only that proportion of children whose early home life has been reasonably secure and happy and who are also sound both in intelligence and temperament could be sent to Southern Rhodesia.[11]

The reports emphasize the importance of the children's reasonably secure emotional background, their relative intellect and also, implicitly, their class background; the selected children were most often from lower middle-class or working class families, rather than from the most down and out portion of the population. The recollections of former Fairbridgians reveal, however, that their childhood homes were often not as stable and their backgrounds not necessarily as secure as the scheme's publicity material would indicate. In fact, as the immediate post-war years passed, it became more and more difficult for the Council to obtain children who would fit the tight requirements. This eventually – along with changed conceptions of child welfare and the looming independence of British colonies – led to the gradual dissolving of the scheme. Thus, as one moves from the pages of publicity brochures and committee memoranda to the narratives of the migrant children, a different story line emerges. Very often the children came from single-parent families or stepfamilies. The life stories also disclose that the intentions for emigration were rarely transparent to the children themselves.

'My mother told me various stories', said Helen,[12] who was sent to Rhodesia in 1952 when she was 6 years old. 'I probably still don't know the truth (...) but what she did maintain all the time was that she did it for our education. That's what she always came back to. She did it for our education.' 'Mother always referred to herself as having itchy feet', said Leslie, who was born in 1947 and migrated to Rhodesia at the age of seven. He continues:

> [Mother] always said she thought she was doing this for the best, but I was always a little cynical and unforgiving about that. I suspect stepfather wanted only his own kids (...) The separation from our mother took place at Waterloo Station as the boat train left, and was marked by an air of forced jollity (...) Didn't know anything about Southern Rhodesia or Africa. We found that out when we got there to our own little Britain in the Bush.

Bringing up new Rhodesians

> A total institution may be defined as a place of residence and work where a large number of like situated individuals, cut off from the wider society for an appreciable period of time, together lead an enclosed, formally administered round of life. (Goffman 1961, xiii)

According to Erving Goffman, an elementary social arrangement in a modern (western) society is that 'the individual tends to sleep, play, and work in different places, with different co-participants, under different authorities, and without an over-all rational plan' (1961, 5–6). A total institution, in contrast, breaks down such barriers. Thus, in a total institution all aspects and activities of life are conducted in a single place and under the same authority. The encompassing character of a total institution is confirmed by the degree to which the place is separated and isolated from the rest of the society and how it physically confines the inmates, limiting their control of personal space, time and material possessions (Goffman 1961, 4). The daily activities are carried out in the company of a 'large batch of others, all of whom are treated alike and required to do the same thing together' (Goffman 1961, 6). Further, the daily activities follow a tight schedule imposed from above. Finally, these activities are compiled into a 'single rational plan purportedly designed to fulfill the official aims of the institution' (Goffman 1961, 6). Goffman's classic characterization of a total institution illuminates significant aspects of the structures of everyday life at Fairbridge College.[13]

Faribridge College was established on a 1200-acre property. Its facilities included a gymnasium, a cricket pitch, swimming pool, tennis and squash courts, and a chapel. The children were housed in gender-segregated dormitories with 12–14 children in each. They attended a co-educational primary school at the premises of the College, following the Rhodesian curriculum until the age of 11, after which they attended secondary schools in the nearby town of Bulawayo, where they mixed with local white Rhodesian children. The object of educating the migrants together with local children aimed at making them 'young Rhodesian citizens from their earliest days in the country.'[14]

The daily routine of the college appears so fixed and anchored in memory that the former migrants have no trouble recalling its smallest details today. At junior school: wake up at six, flag parade, breakfast, classes until lunch, afternoon rest, free time, bath, supper, and lights out at seven. 'The bell in the morning went at six o'clock', said Helen, 'and then you got dressed, you washed and brushed your teeth.' After washing up, the children assembled around the flagpole, where 'faces, necks, ears and behind the ears, wrists, hands and fingernails were inspected', as John Neal recalls in his autobiography (Windows 2001, 123). 'We would all stand in our line, the flag would go up, and oh, it was all terribly colonial', Helen reflected. After the flag parade, it was time for breakfast, which was preceded by the saying of grace.

For many Fairbridgians, food memories are intensely vivid and tangible. 'Food seemed to dominate our lives, we were always hungry', writes Jean Norton (Windows 2001, 200). Graham recalled how the children yearned for sugar and sweets in particular:

> I always remember the one chap at Northley [senior school in Bulawayo] he had a Crunchy [chocolate bar] with him. Took his Crunchy out, took it out of the paper, licked it, and said: 'Anyone wanna bite?' Knowing that no other child will, [after] he had licked it. But Fairbridge boys, they'd say: 'Yes, thanks!'

After classes and lunch, the children had to rest for an hour, during which time they were required to lie on their beds in the dorms. They could sleep or read, as long as there was no talking or moving about. After rest, there was either an hour or so of lessons or the children were free until bath time, which was supervised by the housemother. Lights out was at seven, preceded by saying the Lord's Prayer, kneeling by the bedside.

Goffman suggests that 'authority in total institutions is directed to a multitude of items of conduct – dress, deportment, manners – that constantly occur and constantly come up for judgment' (1961, 41). At Fairbridge, the children's comportment, posture, movement, tidiness and cleanliness were monitored by the staff and regulated by the structured organization of time. The schedule determined largely where each child was situated at any given time and what activity they were occupied with. Discipline was readily enforced by corporeal punishment. Helen remembers an event from her first week at Fairbridge:

> I remember the first Friday. I'd been there a week. I remember I got out of my bed and went to talk to somebody and then I could hear this thundering up the dormitory. The matron was a very big woman and it was wooden floors and you could hear everything. She came thundering up towards me, I turned around and she went like that [shows how the woman hit her face with an open hand]. BANG. She hit me. And I, I left the ground. I was here and I landed in there. 'You get out of your bed, you make it. You've been here a week now. You get out of your bed, you make it.' A bit of a wakeup call! I make my bed now. I've always made my bed. Even in a hotel when I'm travelling, I have to consciously make myself not to.

Helen's ordeal exemplifies Goffman's analysis of how the newcomers to an institution are first made aware of their deference obligations. It also exemplifies how certain practices and a sense of uniform orderliness become habitual. In her analysis of British boarding school education, Judith Okeley refers to the training of children's bodies as the 'curriculum of the unconscious' (1996, 139). She argues that bodily lessons may be taught without the pupils' intellectual collaboration; they become embodied and held in memory, held so firmly that Helen, now in her mid-60s, had to consciously make herself to be disobedient.

At primary school, the children were almost completely cut off from the outside world during the school year. They slept and ate, were schooled and played at the premises, which were 'in the bush.' According to Michel Foucault, discipline sometimes requires enclosure, 'a specification of a place (...) closed upon itself (...) a protected place of disciplinary monotony' (1995 [1975], 141). Boarding school appears a prime example of such enclosure. At Fairbridge, the separation from the outside world became all the more pronounced since the children were removed from their homes and homeland. However, true to the boarding school tradition (e.g. Buettner 2004, 130–139), the children maintained their relationship with their parents in a regulated manner by weekly letter writing. Helen recalls this practice vividly:

> On a Sunday we had to go to girls' prep room, and write a letter to our parents. I remember the first occasion, the same matron sat at the front, and I can remember sitting in the room at this desk and I wrote this letter to our mother. I don't know what I said. (...) But what I do remember is, I went to the front, because you had to show [the matron] the letter, and she looked at it, and she read it, and she said: 'Oh no! Oh no', she said 'your mummy doesn't want to hear about things like that! Go and try again.' So I went and sat down, a bit confused. But you know I was in a situation where I had no control at all. I didn't understand where I was and didn't know why I was there. I was just six years old. I had no idea about anything. So I went back and sat down at the desk (...) and I wrote: 'Dear mummy! I am well and happy' which I wasn't 'and how are you?' I am well and happy and how are you? And I started every letter like that in the next ten years. And I wrote rubbish. I

didn't make things up. I just wrote superficial things and she wrote as superficial back to me.[15]

Helen remembers spending her first years at Fairbridge 'in a state of trying to catch up and work out what the hell was happening.' Her solution to the letter writing shows how quickly she had internalized the one key rule in the life at Fairbridge: you had to 'suck it up.' To express any negative feelings was out of the question, unwise and useless. 'If you were upset, you were ridiculed', she continued, 'you would have to tough it out. I think it created, fostered, and developed huge independence but also did damage, huge damage. Some of us more than others.' The sense of independence Helen presents was built on learning to control one's emotions and especially to hide any signs of vulnerability or weakness. This emotional self-restraint and reserve, continuously described by former Fairbridgians, is of course a familiar characterization of the British public school code of conduct. Accordingly, in his analysis of British public schools as agents of imperialism, P. J. Rich (1991, 94) cites E. M. Foster's observation: 'It was not that an Englishman couldn't feel, but that he had been taught at public school that feeling was bad form.'

Self-restraint, independence and self-reliance were key educational aims at Fairbridge. But in addition to learning to control one's vulnerability in the face of others, independence was intriguingly sought by institutionalizing a considerable amount of freedom of movement into the educational scheme and daily routine. The children were free and unsupervised in the afternoon, most of the weekends and nearly all of the holidays. They could run around the surrounding countryside, exploring and moving about at their own will – without any purposeful duties to be accomplished. Unlike in the parades or in sport, their movements, postures and bodily comportments were neither forced nor controlled.

The intention of the Fairbridge scheme – as has been brought out – was to raise the migrant children into committed Rhodesian settler citizens. Significantly, the commitment was grounded in establishing a sense of inclusion and entitlement to the land. The Fairbridge children were socialized into Rhodesian settler ways of belonging to the land by allowing the children to create individual bonds of knowledge, care and love for the landscape. By roaming around through 'the wide open spaces', by learning to know the contours and characters of the landscape and their own ways in it, the children formed an affective relationship with the land, which was considered constitutive in the making of settler citizens (Uusihakala 2008; Hughes 2010). In the former Fairbridgians' recollections, the topic of freedom predominates. 'My overriding thought is of freedom,' writes Catherine Maunder, 'walking to Thabas Induna with a friend, just so as you had a packed lunch and a hat. Those were the days when we were as dirty and disreputable as the boys – we built mud brick shacks [and] brewed tea on open fires' (Windows, 51). Another writer concurs:

In retrospect, it is amazing how much freedom we were given. (…) We got to know the Matabele bush very well. From the old airstrip up to the basalt topped sandstone hill called Thaba Zinduna (hill of the chiefs and site of Mzilikazi's first royal kraal), the world was ours to explore. (Michael Davies, Windows 2001, 61)

Graham too marvelled at the amount of freedom the children were given to wander about in the bush; if the children did not spend their school holidays with a Rhodesian family but stayed at Fairbridge, they were allowed to go camping and could spend an entire week on their own in the bush. In addition to indicating liberty and autonomy, Graham also regarded this freedom as lack of care and a sign of abandonment, wondering why the children had bothered to return from their journeys, since nobody seemed to care, one way or the other.

Installing a sense of freedom and ownership of the landscape corresponds to the positions the children were expected to occupy in the society as they grew up (see also Boucher 2014). In the white Rhodesian conceptualization, the pioneering ideals of enterprise, freedom, and opportunity, were, time and again, discursively carved into the concept of *open country*, which seemed to elicit a sense of possession, a feeling that 'the country belonged to you' (Uusihakala 2008, 86). Thus, whereas the Australian migrants on Fairbridge schemes were taught domestic chores and farm work, and their daily schedules were elaborate and strictly supervised, in Rhodesia it was paramount that the children developed a sense of belonging to the land through institutionalized freedom inscribed in the curriculum.

Conclusion

We lived in a microcosm that had likened itself to some form of English public school, we saw ourselves as special, and an elite. But we were a part of an inappropriate experiment, placed out of step with time, in a society that still had colonial ambitions, whilst the Empire was being dismantled about us. (Vivian Finn, Windows 2001, 217)

As a Goffmanian total institution, the Fairbridge College sought to socialize the children into good Rhodesian citizens by strict spatiotemporal design; first, by partially cutting them off from the rest of the society and binding them to the confines of the institution, and second, by structuring the schedule by which the children's daily life followed an unwavering routine. But Goffman's argumentation about what total institutions do is not altogether in accordance with Fairbridge ambitions in regard to upbringing. According to Goffman: 'Total institutions disrupt or defile precisely those actions that in civil society have the role of attesting to the actor and those in his presence that he has some command over his world – that he is a person with "adult" self-determination, autonomy, and freedom of action' (1961, 43). The Fairbridge educational scheme appears more ambiguous than that. Although the freeness of time inscribed in the curriculum was arguably limited – it was punctuated by the bell and had its determined place in the schedule – it was time that was not monitored by any authorities. It was time to be made by the children's initiative, with the aim of 'instilling self-determination, autonomy, and freedom of action' in the children, and thus preparing them for the positions in the social hierarchy, which they were meant to occupy in the future. Importantly, this freedom of movement worked to create a commitment to the locality while indicating simultaneously broader educational objectives of imperial mobile identity.

I began this article by citing two quotes from the Fairbridge Scholars' website. The first one pronounces the official intent of the migration scheme, defining the migrant children as worthy investments, the profits of which were seen to benefit the entire Empire. The second citation reflects the outcome: the invested child's frustrated response at not having been able to influence or even to understand the drastic turn of one's life's course. Examination of the Fairbridge scheme thus enables one to consider how strategies and aims of migration are connected in particular ways with aspirations and hopes related both to individual goals, as well as to broader, social and political objectives. In this case, the migration scheme intended to benefit the individual children by rescuing and removing them from what were predicted as undesirable futures and offering them instead, through emigration and education, a potential for social advancement. The advantages of the migratory project were to reach beyond the individual children, who in the grand scheme of things were a means of rescuing the Empire by keeping it civilized and British.

It is no surprise that the outcomes of the project are more complicated than its intentions. The selected children were meant to sustain a colonial social order, which was soon to fall apart. Intended to be brought up into committed settler citizens, few Fairbridgians ended up staying in Zimbabwe.[16] In that respect, they followed the emigration streams of other white Rhodesians, the largest numbers of whom migrated from Zimbabwe in the early 1980s. However, the formation of a mobile colonial identity was also intrinsic to the migration scheme and its educational aims, and in this sense the Fairbridgians in their onward movements realized the plan. But although the mobile life histories might indicate an ability to be at home in any corner of the Empire, many Fairbridgians consider that they lack a deep sense of belonging anywhere. The loyalty and commitment which does emerge is that towards their peers – the fellow Fairbridgians, who have shared their experience of migration and growing up in a place that, as such, no longer exists. The Fairbridge experience, therefore, offers an example of how unpredictable, tangled and complex the outcomes of projects of colonial social engineering might well be.

Notes

1. Outline of the Scheme 1939. D 296/K2/4/1, (ULSCA).
2. Ellen Boucher situates modern child emigration in the Victorian child rescue move ment which was grounded on a conviction that children needed to be educated and

freed from the burden of labor and that these ideals should be extended to the laboring poor (2009, 917 918, 2014). See also Grier (2002), Paul (2001), Harper and Constantine (2010).

3. The exact number of child migrants is difficult to ascertain. Boucher (2014) and Harper and Constantine (2010, 248) estimate that from 1869 until the late 1960s roughly 95,000 children were permanently relocated in the settler dominions.

4. The research is supported by the Kone Foundation post doctoral research grant.

5. The territory of Southern Rhodesia became part of the British Empire in 1890 when it was conquered by the British South Africa Company. It gained a status of a self governing colony in 1923. In 1953 Southern Rhodesia joined Northern Rhodesia and Nyasaland to form a Federation. Towards the end of the 1950s African resistance to white minority rule grew vocal and the Federation dissolved in 1963, followed by Northern Rhodesia's independence as Zambia and Nyasaland's as Malawi. The nationalist movements in Southern Rhodesia also demanded independence, while the white populist Rhodesian Front party campaigned for the continuity of white rule. In 1965, Ian Smith, the leader of Rhodesian Front, declared the country unilaterally independent. The UDI was followed by almost two decades of civil war between the nationalist movements and the white ruled Rhodesian state. Zimbabwe finally became independent in 1980. An estimated 100,000 whites emi grated from the country during the first years of independence.

6. Publicity brochure, May 1948. D 296/K2/3/2, (ULSCA).

7. D 296/K2/4/2, (ULSCA).

8. The white population rose from 1,500 in 1891 to about 70,000 in 1941 and 232,000 in 1979. Whites remained a clear minority throughout the colonial rule; Africans outnumbered Europeans by approximately twenty to one (Kennedy 1987; Lowry 2010). While trying to attract the 'right kind' of immigrants, Rhodesia also actively restricted immigration. Prospective settlers needed to have employment or sufficient capital to prevent the problem of 'poor whites'. But, according to Mlambo (2000, 141), what mattered most in defining the right type of migrant was not wealth but the 'being of British stock.'

9. D 296/K2/1/2, (ULSCA).

10. Legislative Assembly meeting, 28 October 1937. DO 35 844/7, (TNA).

11. Proposed Establishment of a Fairbridge Farm School, 3 September 1938. DO 35/ 697/5, (TNA).

12. I use pseudonyms to protect the identity of my informants. Real names of the authors are used for published texts.

13. Christie Davies (1989) has further developed Goffman's concept. She considers (1) the degree of openness or closedness, (2) the explicit purpose and (3) the dominant mode of eliciting compliance in various institutions. Accordingly, Fairbridge College may be considered an intermediate total institution, because the pupils were, in theory, free to enter or leave the institution, and they could aspire to move in the internal social hierarchy. Secondly, the purpose of the institution was to transform its inmates (rather than to lock them away) into 'useful or at any rate conforming adults' (Davies 1989, 88). Thirdly, the dominant mode of compliance was normative, not coercive or remunerative (Davies 1989, 90).

14. A promotional booklet, 1954. D 296/K2/4/5, (ULSCA).

15. It needs to be said that some Fairbridgians did find letter writing meaningful. Catherine Maunder, for example, writes: 'I had ample proof of [mother's] love when I discovered that she had kept every letter, card, school report and photo that I had ever sent her. My life was there, laid out in an old leather trunk' (Windows 2001, 53).

16. According to a student list provided by one of my informants, of the slightly over 100 former Fairbridgians whose place of residence was known in 2013, close to 30% live in the United Kingdom, nearly 30% in South Africa and 30% in Australia and New Zealand. Only four people were known to still live in Zimbabwe. About 20% of former Fairbridgians are known to be deceased.

References

BBC News. 2010. "Gordon Brown Apologizes to Child Migrants Sent Abroad." *BBC News*, February 24. Accessed May 27, 2013. http://news.bbc.co.uk/2/hi/8531664.stm

Boucher, E. 2009. "The Limits of Potential: Race, Welfare, and the Interwar Extension of Child Emigration to Southern Rhodesia." *The Journal of British Studies* 48 (4): 914 934. doi:10.1086/603596.

Boucher, E. 2014. *Empire's Children: Child Emigration and Child Welfare in the British World, 1969 1967*. Cambridge: Cambridge University Press.

Buettner, E. 2004. *Empire Families: Britons and Late Imperial India*. Oxford: Oxford University Press.

Challis, R. J. 1982. *The European Educational System in Southern Rhodesia 1890 1930*. Supplement *to Zambezia*. Salisbury: University of Zimbabwe.

Davies, C. 1989. "Goffman's Concept of the Total Institution: Criticisms and Revisions." *Human Studies* 12 (1 2): 77 95. doi:10.1007/BF00142840.

Foucault, M. 1995 [1975]. *Discipline and Punish: The Birth of the Prison*. New York: Vintage Books.

Goffman, E. 1961. *Asylums: Essays on the Social Situation of Mental Patients and Other Inmates*. New York: Anchor Books.

Grier, J. 2002. "Voluntary Rights and Statutory Wrongs: The Case of Child Migration, 1948 67." *History of Education* 31 (3): 263 280. doi:10.1080/00467600210122621.

Harper, M. and S. Constantine. 2010. *Migration and Empire*. Oxford: Oxford University Press.

Hughes, D. 2010. *Whiteness in Zimbabwe: Race, Landscape, and the Problem of Belonging*. New York: Palgrave Macmillan.

Kennedy, D. 1987. *Islands of White: Settler Society and Culture in Kenya and Southern Rhodesia, 1890 1939*. Durham: Duke University Press.

Kingsley Fairbridge Scholars Reunion Webpage. 2002. Accessed March 23, 2012. http://www.fairbridge worldwide.com

Lowry, D. 2010. "Rhodesia 1890 1980: 'The Lost Dominion'." In *Settlers and Expatriates: Britons over the Seas*, edited by R. Bickers, 112 149. Oxford: Oxford University Press.

Mlambo, A. S. 2000. "Some Are More White than Others": Racial Chauvinism as a Factor in Rhodesian Immigration Policy, 1890 to 1963." *Zambezia* XXVII (ii): 139 160.

Okely, J. 1996. *Own or Other Culture*. London: Routledge.

Paul, K. 2001. "Changing Childhoods: Child Emigration since 1945." In *Child Welfare and Social Action in the Nineteenth and Twentieth Centuries*, edited by J. Lawrence and P. Starkey, 121 144. Liverpool: Liverpool University Press.

Rich, P. J. 1991. *Chains of Empire: English Public Schools, Masonic Cabalism, Historical Causality, and Imperial Clubdom*. London: Regency Press.

Sherington, G. and C. Jeffery. 1998. *Fairbridge: Empire and Child Migration*. London: Woburn Press.

Stoler, A. L. 1989. "Rethinking Colonial Categories: European Communities and the Boundaries of Rule." *Comparative Studies in Society and History* 31 (1): 134 161. doi:10.1017/S0010417500015693.

Summers, C. 1994. *From Civilization to Segregation: Social Ideals and Social Control in Southern Rhodesia, 1890 1934*. Athens: University of Ohio Press.

Uusihakala, K. 2008. *Memory Meanders: Place, Home and Commemoration in an Ex Rhodesian Diaspora Community*. Helsinki: University of Helsinki Press.

Windows, 2001. *Windows: Rhodesia Fairbridge Memorial College Autobiographies*. Christchurch: Fairbridge Marketing Company.

Archival collections (UK)

The National Archives, Public Record Office, Kew (TNA)

University of Liverpool, Special Collections and Archives, Liverpool (ULSCA)

Gendered educational trajectories and transnational marriage among West African students in France

Hélène Neveu Kringelbach

French colonialism resulted in the inclusion of large numbers of West Africans into French educational institutions. Furthermore, the Senegambian region has a long history of intermarriage with French citizens. This paper draws on this history to explore the interplay between migration, education and binational marriage over several generations of West African students, with a particular focus on Senegal. Students from Francophone countries continue to seek educational opportunities in France, but in recent years they have been increasingly affected by the tightening up of immigration policies. In this context, this paper suggests that marriage to a French spouse often plays an important role in the fulfilment of educational projects, and that this role is contingent on issues of gender and class. At times, however, tensions between marriage in France and social expectations back home end up compromising education altogether.

In 2012–2013, 12% of the student population enrolled in higher education in France were international students (Campus France 2013). This placed France as the third country behind the US and the UK for its number of international students, with 7% of the total worldwide. There is indeed growing international mobility in the search for degrees, and the reproduction of elites is thus becoming globalised (Findlay et al. 2012). In the major receiving countries, universities are competing to attract international students, in large part for the financial contribution they make as state subsidies dwindle (King and Raghuram 2013). But students do not simply move to get degrees, and there is growing scholarly recognition that educational mobility is part of a broader life course. Yet European states still treat international students as temporary guests whose right to work or establish themselves should be curtailed. This is as much out of fear that they might swell the numbers of 'labour migrants' as out of concern for their education (Raghuram 2013). The role of states in encouraging or restricting access has been well documented, but so far the role of marriage to a citizen or resident in facilitating incorporation into receiving countries has received scant attention. Drawing on material collected for a study on transnational families between Senegal, France and the UK, this article seeks to address the gap in understanding the relationship between migration, transnational marriage and education. I take an anthropological perspective, thus keeping sight of life-course events and culturally constructed ideas on 'education'. I suggest that the role marriage plays in educational migration is not only contingent on immigration policies but also on issues of gender, class and histories of migration.

New immigration policies curtailing the possibility for international students to acquire longer term residency caused massive protest during Nicolas Sarkozy's presidential mandate. In May 2011, French Interior Minister Claude Guéant issued a memo instructing government agencies to limit the number of visa renewals for non-European Union (EU) students and to curtail their right to work after graduating. Although these measures were abandoned by François Hollande's government in 2012, the status of international students in France remains fragile. In this context, marriage to a resident or citizen may play an important role in fulfilling educational projects by granting new rights and eventually citizenship. This is the case in France, where spouse citizenship has historically been awarded fairly generously, albeit under conditions of 'integration' (Hajjat 2012). However, the passage to another life stage may also conflict with education.

This article focuses on Senegal since it was the first West African territory to be incorporated into the French education system. As a result, Senegal has long provided the biggest contingent of sub-Saharan African students in France. In 2012–2013, they represented nearly 14% of sub-Saharan Africans enrolled in public or state-recognised institutions, with 8995 individuals (Campus France 2013). This is a comparatively high figure in relation to Senegal's modest size,[1] and to the documented Senegalese population in France: 98,527 in 2006 (Beauchemin, Caarls, and Mazzucato 2013).

This paper draws on approximately nine months of fieldwork in France and two months in Senegal between 2011 and 2013. Research was conducted through semi-structured interviews, informal conversations and voluntary work with a French civic association providing legal mentoring for bi-national couples, *Les Amoureux au Ban Public*. The material was collected with family relationships and immigration issues in mind, and not with a focus on education. However, education often ranked high in people's aspirations. The broader study includes approximately 50 couples, 12 of whom are separated. There is an equal number of Francophone African men and women and their French spouses. Two-thirds of the couples were recruited using the snowballing method, and the remainder through the 22 evening-long legal advice sessions and social events I attended with the association in Paris. Individuals ranged in age from their twenties to their eighties. This is not a representative sample, and therefore the findings presented here cannot be generalised. My own identity as the child of a French mother and Senegalese father has facilitated access, but may also have skewed testimonies towards the more positive aspects of bi-national marriage. All informant names are pseudonyms.

Conceptualising student mobility, life course and gender

Following an enduring concern with the relationship between education and class, studies of spatial mobility and education have often focused on whether student mobility enabled individuals to achieve the upward mobility they sought (Waters 2006; Biao and Shen 2009; Rao 2010; Brooks and Waters 2011). Following the recent surge in international student mobility, however, a body of literature is emerging, which looks at students not simply as individuals engaged in the pursuit of degrees, but also as endowed with multiple identities (Waters 2006; Baas 2010). In this perspective, educational choices are part of broader aspirations, not simply to social mobility but also to achieving various individual-, family- and class-based projects (Brooks and Everett 2008). Findlay et al. (2012), for example, found that the desire to qualify for long-term residency and citizenship was an explicit motivation for some British students in Australia, and Baas (2006) found that male Indian students in Australia considered marriage as an option to access permanent residency.

With a few exceptions (e.g. Olwig 2007; Valentin 2012), this literature rarely engages with the historical patterns of educational mobility induced by colonialism and other radical shifts. Historical studies on educational mobility in colonial empires have often focused on the political awakening of colonised youths in the metropolitan nations (Guimont 1997; Adi 1998; Dieng 2003; Vaillant 2006). On the whole, however, these studies have not dealt with family relationships. In his work on African intellectuals in France, Guèye (2001, 2002) mentions that many students have married French women, but focused on their political engagement. Though there is no space to do justice to the historical dimension of French–West African marriage here, I adopt a diachronic perspective to draw out the class-based, gendered and intergenerational aspects of the relationship between marriage and educational mobility in a post-colonial context.

This article also engages with the burgeoning literature on transnational marriage (e.g. Bryceson and Vuorela 2002; Constable 2005a; Cole 2010; Bloch 2011; Charsley 2012, 2013; Fernandez 2013). In recent years, this work has shown how states have increasingly policed marriage across national boundaries in an effort to control human mobility. Scholars have also sought to disrupt popular ideas about the commodification of love and sex that is assumed to be at the heart of unions between individuals from wealthier and poorer countries, and this article also points to more nuanced interpretations of cross-border marriage. What does not often appear is that cross-border marriage can involve circulation in both directions. Much has been written on 'global hypergamy' (Constable 2005b) or women crossing regional or national boundaries to marry into wealthier localities or families. The Senegalese case, by contrast, involves both men *and* women 'marrying out'. As Constable (2005b, 19) points out, 'hypergamy begs the question of how, for whom, and in what sense such marriages represent upward mobility'. In Senegal, marriage between African men and French women has become part of the kinship repertoire. Since the 1980s, the gender structure of 'mixed marriage' has shifted with a rise in the proportion of women among Senegalese migrants (Selly Baro 2005). Thus, in 2011 in France, 321 Senegalese men married French women, while 202 Senegalese women married French men (INSEE 2012).[2] This does not include marriages celebrated in Senegal or elsewhere. To what extent and for whom, then, do French–West African marriages represent upward mobility?

Finally, the migration/education/marriage nexus begs the question of the relationship between spatial and social mobility. As established by geographers, and taken up by Olwig and Sørensen (2002), Valentin (2012) and others in the anthropological study of 'mobile livelihoods', social and spatial mobility are interrelated social processes. Spatial mobility, here, is conceived of as the capacity to travel freely through access to financial resources and visas. Social mobility should be understood as a combination of wealth, social status and lifestyle. Throughout West Africa, social mobility has been linked to travel and return with accumulated resources, often in the form of household dependents and the capacity to mobilise the labour of others; this is the notion of 'wealth in people' discussed in classical anthropological texts of the region (e.g. Meillassoux 1981). Men usually had the best access to mobility, while women often held ritual and spiritual power. However, in some parts of the region, such as the Casamance, the cash cropping and waged labour introduced during the colonial period led unmarried women to travel seasonally for work and trade, and to accumulate household goods (Linares 1992; Lambert 2002). Social mobility through spatial mobility, therefore, has historically been gendered. If anything, the rise in migration to France through the twentieth century has reinforced the association between upward mobility and travel to return with increased resources. But downward mobility is always a risk, particularly since the high cost of travel means that those who migrate may have incurred debts. This was already the case in the nineteenth and early twentieth centuries, when the mobility of the Soninke from the Senegal River Valley involved reciprocity among the more privileged groups (Manchuelle 1997). In the region, social mobility through travel is more likely to be achieved by those who already have resources in wealth and social capital.

Creole societies and educational mobility between West Africa and France

From the seventeenth century onwards, coastal Senegal has had a significant French presence, first via traders and later colonial administrators and military officers. A number of the early traders had relationships with African women. The *Compagnie du Sénégal* which employed them encouraged this since it improved their knowledge of the local languages, trading networks and their survival rates (White 1999). Their creole descendants often held important positions in the transatlantic and regional trades, and were among the first to attend the Catholic mission schools established from the eighteenth century onwards. These early developments account for the comparative success of the Senegalese in French formal education. The first Black African representative at the French National Assembly, Blaise Diagne, was thus born on the creolised island of Gorée around 1872, and went to primary school in Saint-Louis before attending secondary school in France. In later generations, President Senghor and others joined the elite after following similarly mobile trajectories. Longer periods of study in France were usually preceded by regional mobility to attend French schools.

The colonial period also transformed notions of an 'educated person'. Ideas about educated persons, as the volume by Levinson, Foley, and Holland (1996) shows, are socially constructed. In the Senegambian region,[3] the notion of a knowledgeable person had long been linked to hereditary status and to the successful completion of initiation cycles (Diop 1985). Islamic education also played an important role in the families of clerics in the pre-colonial period and spread to all social categories during the nineteenth century (Diouf 1990). By leading to posts in the colonial administration for those who held French degrees, colonial schooling heavily promoted formal education. After World War II, the need to reward the colonies for their participation in the war effort was recognised, and growing numbers of young Africans were awarded scholarships to study in France. From 2000 students in 1949–1950, the numbers grew to 8000 in 1959, one-third of whom benefited from French studentships (Guimont 1997, 7). But the studentships undermined the prestige of emerging African universities since French degrees became the reward for a faultless trajectory (Guèye 2002). Many among the post-war generations returned to their home countries to take up high-ranking positions in the late colonial administration, and after 1960 in the newly independent states. French colonialism, then, inscribed a durable connection between migration, foreign degrees and social mobility. In Senegal, this connection was reinforced in the 1980s, when a succession of student strikes in Dakar rendered the local university even less attractive (Guèye 2002). In contemporary Senegal therefore, an educated person is, to a large extent, a person with degrees, preferably from foreign institutions.

In the 1950s, African students in Paris socialised around the Latin Quarter, where they went to cafés and evening dances with French women, many of whom were from provincial towns. Several women I interviewed had fond memories of these impeccably turned out black men who spoke of revolutionising their home countries. They wore suits to distinguish themselves from migrant 'workers', and to fend off an ever-present racism. As some of the women confessed, meeting educated men from faraway countries was all the more exciting as they themselves were regarded as 'migrants' from smaller French towns. This colonial context helps to explain the historical propensity of Francophone African students, especially Senegalese, to marry French women. Two additional factors played into this: the difficulties African students faced in securing accommodation and the scarcity of studentships. Indeed in the 1950s, in a context of militant anti-colonialism, the French state withdrew the scholarships of those African students deemed too militant or too fickle in their choice of a subject (Dieng 2003). After the Independencies in 1960, studentships became a strategic instrument in France's relations with its former colonies. Since Senegal and Côte d'Ivoire remained France's closest allies in West Africa, students from these countries enjoyed comparatively favourable treatment. Nevertheless, by the mid-1970s studentships had become scarcer, and living conditions in France had deteriorated. Indeed, racial discrimination meant that African students faced huge difficulties in securing housing, an enduring problem to this day (Coulon and Paivandi 2003).

Dual citizenship and social mobility in the post-Independence years

In this context, marriage to French women often enabled university education to be completed in better conditions. One must be careful, however, not to reduce these relationships to instrumental arrangements, as evident in the substantial number of relationships of more than 10 years which I have come across. Here, I focus on the generations who came of age between the 1950s and the 1970s.

For Senegalese students, there was an aura of elitism in bi-national marriage, even though not every Senegalese shared this view. Indeed several informants from different generations reported being warned before departure: 'Come back with degrees, not with a French woman!' Some of the reluctance expressed had to do with the fear of 'losing a child to France', especially in families where individuals from earlier generations had married in France and never returned. For those who could not claim French citizenship at Independence or who chose not to, marriage later offered an alternative, and several of my older informants became French through marriage. They have remained dual nationals, and have often enjoyed better professional opportunities than their peers. As visas became required from the 1970s onwards, they also had the advantage of a greater spatial mobility, which contributed to their social mobility. The father of one of my informants is thus a Senegalese civil servant who married a French woman while a student in France in the 1970s. He acquired French citizenship through marriage and kept his Senegalese citizenship alongside. His wife completed her studies and then worked to support the family, enabling him to do further graduate work. They eventually divorced and he remarried a Senegalese woman, who in turn acquired French citizenship by marrying him. He enjoyed a long career as a French diplomat before drawing on his dual nationality to return to Senegal and take part in Macky Sall's new government in 2012. Marriage greatly facilitated his education and his subsequent high-profile career.

Marriage into French families also enabled these individuals to learn about French cultural practices first-hand. Although intermarriage between citizens and immigrants does not always foster social incorporation (cf. Song 2009), there has long been a strong perception, in France, that the two were connected.[4] Findlay et al. (2012, 128) rightly point out that international student mobility is not only about gaining formal knowledge, but 'also about other socially and culturally constructed knowledges'. How this happens in everyday life is rarely described in the literature on student mobility. Yet the cultural knowledge acquired from spending time with French in-laws came to the fore in my informants' testimonies, across all generations. For Senegalese individuals, incorporation into a new social context is often understood within a model of tutor–guest relationship, which involves the initial protection of someone in whose household one may live for as long as it takes to establish oneself. In return, 'guests' remain indebted to their tutors once they have established their own household. Though this is obviously an ideal that is not always practised, it did affect the expectations young Senegalese had when marrying into French families.

Sadly however, rejection by French families was quite common. African students in France often came from middle-class backgrounds, and it was particularly painful to be rejected by in-laws they regarded as no superior to their own relatives. In practice, families on both sides were often divided, with some members looking favourably upon the unions, and others showing hostility, even racism. For West African Muslims, religious difference was an additional issue. Indeed in some French Catholic families, the spouse's parents had looked forward to church weddings and Catholic grandchildren. But family relationships often improved if the African spouse was successful professionally. A couple who met in the early 1960s thus explained how the parents of the French wife, Jacqueline, went from complete rejection of the Senegalese (Muslim) husband Seydou to warming to him. They showed this by way of small everyday gestures, such as refraining from serving pork in his presence. Things had not started well, however. During her first pregnancy, Jacqueline had 'fled' to Senegal and waited there for Seydou to finish his studies before taking up a post in a state-owned company. Jacqueline's father was a doctor, and given his hostility to this match, she had feared that he might 'interfere with the pregnancy', as she put it. If transnational marriage facilitated educational projects, individuals often felt that this came at a high personal cost.

In the Senegalese case, until the late 1970s many students returned home, where there was plenty of work for young men with French degrees. Several informants explained that a European wife was the ultimate validation of upward mobility. Some of the white French men who held technical and managerial posts in the Senegalese state sector, however, resented young men like Seydou, who not only competed with them professionally, but also had French wives from 'good' families. These tensions were compounded by the fact that those Senegalese men who had neither foreign degrees nor European wives resented the favourable treatment given to their peers.

Forced immobility and the emergence of women migrants

Since the mid-1970s, French immigration rules have been gradually tightened. Between 2003 and 2011, a succession of laws restricted access for non-EU citizens even further. If anything, this is likely to have made marriage to French citizens even more attractive.

Few students follow a straightforward path in any case, but the trajectories of Francophone African students are further complicated by the fact that they often discover new subjects once in France. Also, a number of informants found that some of the subjects which had appeared promising at home were far less prestigious globally, and had taken new orientations subsequently. But in the past decade, student visas have come under increasing scrutiny, and those who change courses or do not progress fast enough face deportation when their applications for visa renewals are rejected. Indeed, changing course of study places individuals under strong suspicion of being economic migrants posing as international students. In addition, a high proportion of international students face serious financial difficulties (Paivandi 1998). In this context, marriage may help to resume an educational project postponed due to a lack of legal status.

Michelle, a young woman from Gabon, thus told me how she had come to France to study French literature. After a couple of years, she no longer saw much promise in the subject, and enrolled in a more applied subject. Michelle was unable to renew her student visa because her trajectory was deemed 'inconsistent' by the local *Préfecture*. She made ends meet by working in restaurant kitchens at night. But the despair of seeing her education thus compromised led her into depression, which she described as a deep feeling of apathy. She avoided public places and did not feel able to socialise: 'When I lost my papers, I switched myself off from society', she said. She eventually met a young French student with whom she fell in love. They decided to get married, but given her undocumented status, there was immediate suspicion that this might be a 'sham' marriage. The local town hall threatened to report them to the Chief Prosecutor, who might then have requested a police enquiry into their relationship. They eventually got married in the rural locality of her husband's parents, where the mayor was a friend. Michelle subsequently returned to Gabon to apply for a spouse visa from there. Her visa was granted, and she is now considering embarking on a new degree. In retrospect, she does not regret working in restaurant kitchens because she discovered France's 'hidden side' of invisible immigrants. She will apply for French citizenship after the four years of marriage required by French law.

So far, I have only touched on situations in which African students had met their spouse in France. But marriage to a European national encountered at home may also enable individuals to pursue studies in Europe. I use the term 'Europe' here because there is now a much greater diversity of origin countries in bi-national marriage with Francophone Africans, as evident in Rodríguez-García's (2006) illuminating study of Senegalese–Spanish couples in Spain. For obvious language and historical reasons, Francophone African students still come to France in large numbers. But studentships and visas are scarce resources, and marriage may thus offer educational opportunities that would not exist otherwise. In Senegal, this is particularly relevant for young women, who were often, until recently, marginalised in family decisions regarding which children would be schooled. Since the 1980s, access to education has become more balanced, but there remains a gap: in 2011, 45% of boys of secondary school age were enrolled, against 37% of girls; the gap remained in higher education, with 10% and 6%, respectively (UNESCO 2013). For young Senegalese women then, marrying 'out' may be an even more decisive element in pursuing higher education than it is for young men.

In the cases I have encountered where couples had met in Senegal, further education did not necessarily form part of the couple's plans at the time of marriage. But as some later moved to France or elsewhere and faced difficulties in finding employment, they decided that further education for the Senegalese spouse would be beneficial. This is the case of Pierre and Aïda, who met in Senegal when Pierre was employed in the development sector. Aïda was completing a Bachelor's degree in Dakar, and had failed to get a studentship to study in France. They lived in Senegal for a few years before moving to France when Pierre's contract ended. He found employment first, and despite her Senegalese degree, Aïda found it difficult to get qualified jobs. The couple decided that a French degree would give her a better chance, even though there was now a young child, and living on a single salary was a challenge. Aïda embarked on a Masters' course in an applied subject. In the meantime she had acquired French citizenship, and she now qualified for exams to join the civil service. She has been working as a civil servant for several years. Although she feels overqualified for her post, she is grateful for the relative job security citizenship has enabled her to achieve.

I have suggested that for Francophone African students in France, marriage may offer an alternative way of securing educational projects by enabling individuals to live in decent conditions, to avoid the grinding renewal of student visas, and eventually to become French citizens. This, as noted, does not imply that marriage is purely instrumental in such cases, although instrumental reasons are as likely to exist there as in any other marriage. Here, it is worth mentioning the presence of a substantial amount of sex tourism in Senegal and the Gambia, which involves both sexes (Ebron 1997; Fouquet 2007; Salomon 2009). Some of these relationships lead to marriage migration, and an unknown proportion of the Senegambian spouses move into further education once abroad. In coastal Senegambia, therefore, trades such as guides, dancers or musicians have the double advantage of providing livelihoods in the present, and possible migration opportunities in the future (Neveu Kringelbach 2013). None of the longer relationships I have come across, however, could be reduced to migratory projects; rather, in some cases they have turned into marriages earlier than they would have if the couple had not been forced to worry about legal status. But as Froerer and Portisch (2012) remind us, formal education does not always deliver its promises. What role does marriage play in compromised educational trajectories?

Marriage and compromised educational trajectories

Whether or not marriage has positive educational outcomes is not only gendered, but also contingent on age, class, legal status, place and of course individual ability. Thus, by the time people are able to resume truncated educational trajectories, they may find themselves caught up in a web of obligations. West African migrants often find that expectations of remittances increase with the years as families expect success to bear a direct relation to the time spent away. In Senegal, remittances cut across all social classes since they are determined by not only economic need, but also by a reciprocal desire to maintain strong transnational connections (Riccio 2001). But marriage to a French citizen or resident creates a web of obligations of its own, and tensions arise when people must share their resources between family back home and a household in France. The passage to another life stage, then, means that marriage does not always have a positive effect on educational projects.

For Nafissatou, a young Ivorian woman, marriage may have thus come too late. She had left secondary school in Côte d'Ivoire before completing the Baccalaureate and arrived in France in the early 2000s. Côte d'Ivoire was heading for civil war, and her mother was worried that her education may be compromised. Nafissatou came on a tourist visa, but found that this did not allow her to enrol in a state school. Some private schools were happy to turn a blind eye, but the family could not afford them. As Côte d'Ivoire descended deeper into crisis, Nafissatou's mother advised her against going back. Nafissatou remained undocumented for years, and coped by working as a nanny. She shared small flats with friends, moved often to avoid deportation, spent little on herself and sent money home to her mother, who was looking after her own ageing mother. Nafissatou eventually met a French man of her age, and they married the following year. Not only did they have to move a couple of times to find a town hall willing to marry them, but they also endured administrative harassment for a year and a half to get a spouse visa for Nafissatou. By now, Nafissatou says it is too late for her to go back to school. She is still looking after children, and feels she cannot let her mother down by quitting work. She does not, either, wish to be entirely dependent on her husband's income since she feels that his family would then suspect her of marrying him 'for the papers and the money'. Moreover, having her own income enables her to send more money back home. She is considering doing a short training as a nursery worker, but only if this does not prevent her from working simultaneously.

In other cases, failed marriages compromise the legal status and educational opportunities of migrant spouses. For Amadou, a young Senegalese who came to France to study in the mid-2000s, marriage has been an unfortunate distraction. With a Baccalaureate from Senegal, Amadou hurried to France and ignored his mother's advice to complete a first degree at home. He failed his first-year exams and was offered a retake, but in the meantime had become involved with a young French woman whose parents were West African. He decided to move in with her and suspend his studies for a while. His student visa was not renewed, therefore, and marriage became an urgent matter. Although Amadou points out that he was in love, he confesses that the loss of his status hastened the process. The couple found a morally acceptable way of dealing with the urgency by doing a simple civil ceremony, and postponing the Muslim wedding until later. This way, Amadou was able to get a temporary spouse visa while they began the negotiations for the Muslim ceremony. Sadly, the relationship floundered soon after the religious ceremony, which was celebrated in Senegal. They eventually separated, but Amadou's wife went along with the pretence of a married life so that he could renew his visa. To put on the performance for him, he said, she demanded to be paid in cash.

Amadou's parents in Senegal are middle-class, university-educated and practising Muslims. Their priority is for him to get a degree before returning home, and they do not expect to receive remittances just yet. Amadou, for his part, cannot face the prospect of going home empty-handed, especially since his mother had to borrow a significant sum of money for him to study abroad. Like Michelle, he works in restaurant kitchens, and is saving up to enrol in a private engineering course. From his perspective, marriage to a French citizen has undermined his education without giving him access to any rights. Amadou is only one of thousands of African students who go from aspirations of upward mobility to being trapped in a liminal space of immobility, where educational and personal aspirations are put on hold.

Conclusion

I have drawn on several generations of West African students in France to suggest that a focus on marriage sheds light on the relationship between migration, education and social mobility. Two main conclusions can be drawn from the material presented here.

First, understanding the transformative effect of education abroad requires a focus on students as family members, which may include the roles of spouse and parent, rather than as autonomous individuals. This requires paying attention to educational trajectories as part of broader aspirations, a focus that is emerging in the literature on international student mobility. In the case of West African students in France, marriage to a citizen has long played an important role in educational trajectories by providing access to longer term residency, citizenship and an experiential knowledge of French everyday life.

Second, the ways in which transnational marriage shapes educational trajectories is contingent on a range of factors beyond individual abilities, particularly the political context and attitudes towards migrants, historical patterns of mobility and the gender as well as class background of the migrants. In relation to the political context, I have attempted to show how the movement of West African students to France throughout the twentieth century has been encouraged by colonial, then post-colonial educational policies. In the more recent period, these students have become caught up in the tension between France's desire to maintain good relationships with its former colonies and rising anti-immigrant sentiments in France, particularly towards African Muslims. In this context, transnational marriage is likely to play an ever more important role in the fulfilment of educational projects. Where Senegal is concerned, this is in continuity with a history of French colonialism, which imposed a model of success linked to mastery of the French language, migration to acquire degrees and incorporation into the creole coastal elites.

Gender also comes across here as a crucial element in the migration/education/marriage nexus: until the 1980s, it was mainly Senegalese men who benefited from degrees from French higher education institutions, and who married French women. In the past few decades, this gender imbalance has moved towards a gradual reversal with the increase in Senegalese girls' access to schooling and to education abroad. Marriage between Senegalese women students and French men has also been fostered both by encounters in Senegal and by an increase in transnational marriage between Senegal and France, which in some cases involves French men of Senegalese origin.

Finally, class also figures as an important factor because most West Africans who have the opportunity to come to France to study are middle class, often from families with a history of formal education over several generations. However, the cost of living in France and the inability of government studentships to cover living expenses, mean that West African families must often pool resources to send a student abroad. This, in turn, raises expectations that students will work their way through their studies and remit money back home. Failure to achieve this undermines the social status of both students and relatives, just as failure to acquire degrees is associated with downward mobility. In this context, marriage to a citizen may salvage compromised educational projects, but the passage to a new life stage may also undermine them. In any case, the evidence presented here makes a strong case for how educational trajectories both shape and are shaped by transnational marriages and for the salience of colonial histories in international student mobility.

Acknowledgments

I am grateful to the Leverhulme Trust for funding the project on multinational families and new identities this study forms part of, within the Oxford Diaspora Programme (http://www.migration.ox.ac.uk/odp/).

Notes

1. Senegal had an official population of 12.5 million in 2010 (ANSD 2011).
2. The category 'French' includes individuals of Senegalese origin who have acquired citizenship through a first marriage or long term residency.
3. The Senegambian region includes Senegal, the Gambia and the border regions in Mauritania, Mali, Guinea Bissau and Guinea.
4. For scholarly takes on whether the high percentage of 'mixed' marriages in France is indicative of the social incorporation of immigrants, see Collet (1993), Safi (2008) and Tribalat (2009). Also see Todd (1994), Alba and Nee (2005), Song (2009) and Rodríguez García (2012) for broader discussions of the relationship between inter marriage and 'integration'.

References

Adi, H. 1998. *West Africans in Britain, 1900 1960: Nationalism, Pan Africanism, and Communism*. London: Lawrence & Wishart.

Alba, R., and V. Nee. 2005. *Remaking the American Mainstream: Assimilation and Contemporary Immigration*. Cambridge, MA: Harvard University Press.

ANSD. 2011. *Situation économique et sociale du Sénégal en 2010*. Dakar: Agence Nationale de la Démographie et de la Statistique.

Baas, M. 2006. "Students of Migration: Indian Overseas Students and the Question of Permanent Residency." *People and Place* 14 (1), 9 24.

Baas, M. 2010. *Imagined Mobility: Migration and Transnationalism among Indian Students in Australia*. London: Anthem Press.

Beauchemin, C., K. Caarls, and V. Mazzucato. 2013. "Senegalese Migrants between here and there: An Overview of Family Patterns." *MAFE Working Papers*.

Biao, X., and W. Shen. 2009. "International Student Migration and Social Stratification in China." *International Journal of Educational Development* 29: 513 522. doi:10.1016/j.ijedudev.2009.04.006.

Bloch, A. 2011. "Intimate Circuits: Modernity, Migration and Marriage among Post Soviet Women in Turkey." *Global Networks* 11 (4): 502 521. doi:10.1111/j.1471 0374.2011.00303.x.

Brooks, R., and G. Everett. 2008. "The Prevalence of Life Planning: Evidence from UK Graduates." *British Journal of Sociology of Education* 29: 325 337. doi:10.1080/01425690801966410.

Brooks, R., and J. L. Waters. 2011. *Student Mobilities: Migration and the Internationalization of Higher Education*. Basingstoke: Palgrave Macmillan.

Bryceson, D., and U. Vuorela. 2002. *The Transnational Family: New European Frontiers and Global Networks*. Oxford: Berg.

Campus France. 2013. *Les Etudiants Internationaux. Chiffres Clés France 2012 2013: Actualisation*. Paris: Campus France.

Charsley, K. 2012. "Transnational Marriage." In *Transnational Marriage: New Perspectives from Europe and Beyond*, edited by K. Charsley, 3 22. London: Routledge.

Charsley, K. 2013. *Transnational Pakistani Connections: Marrying 'Back Home'*. London: Routledge.

Cole, J. 2010. *Sex and Salvation: Imagining the Future in Madagascar*. Chicago, IL: Chicago University Press.

Collet, B. 1993. "Couples Mixtes En France, Couples Binationaux En Allemagne." *Hommes & Migrations* 1167: 15 19.

Constable, N. 2005a. *Cross Border Marriages: Gender and Mobility in Transnational Asia*. Philadelphia: University of Pennsylvania Press.

Constable, N. 2005b. "Introduction: Cross Border Marriages, Gendered Mobility, and Global Hypergamy." In *Cross Border Marriages: Gender and Mobility in Transnational Asia*, edited by N. Constable, 1 16. Philadelphia: University of Pennsylvania Press.

Coulon, A., and S. Paivandi. 2003. *Les Étudiants Étrangers En France: L'état Des Savoirs. Rapport Pour L'observatoire De La Vie Étudiante*. Paris: Université de Paris 8.

Dieng, A. A. 2003. *Les Premiers Pas De La Fédération Des Etudiants D'afrique Noire En France (1950 1955). De L'union Française À Bandoung*. Paris: L'Harmattan.

Diop, A. B. 1985. *La Famille Wolof*. Paris: Karthala.

Diouf, M. 1990. *Le Kajoor Au XIXe Siècle: Pouvoir Ceddo Et Conquête Coloniale*. Paris: Karthala.

Ebron, P. 1997. "Traffic in Men." In *Gendered Encounters. Challenging Cultural Boundaries and Social Hierarchies in Africa*, edited by M. Grosz Ngate and O. H. Kokole, 223 245. London: Routledge.

Fernandez, N. T. 2013. "Moral Boundaries and National Borders: Cuban Marriage Migration to Denmark." *Identities: Global Studies in Culture and Power* 20 (3): 270 287. doi:10.1080/1070289X.2013.806266.

Findlay, A. M., R. King, F. M. Smith, A. Geddes, and R. Skeldon. 2012. "World Class? An Investigation of Globalisation, Difference and International Student Mobility." *Transactions of the Institute of British Geographers* 37: 118 131. doi:10.1111/j.1475 5661.2011.00454.x.

Fouquet, T. 2007. "De La Prostitution Clandestine Aux Désirs De L'ailleurs: Une 'Ethnographie De L'extraversion' à Dakar." *Politique Africaine* 3 (107): 102 123.

Froerer, P., and A. Portisch 2012. "Introduction to the Special Issue: Learning, Livelihoods, and Social Mobility." *Anthropology and Education Quarterly* 43 (4): 332 343. doi:10.1111/j.1548 1492.2012.01188.x.

Guèye, A. 2001. *Les Intellectuels Africains En France*. Paris: L'Harmattan.

Guèye, A. 2002. "Les Intellectuels Sénégalais En France." In *Le Sénégal Contemporain*, edited by M. C. Diop, 215 240. Paris: Karthala.

Guimont, F. 1997. *Les Etudiants Africains En France (1950 1965)*. Paris: L'Harmattan.

Hajjat, A. 2012. *Les Frontières De L'identité Nationale*. Paris: La Découverte.

INSEE. 2012. "Mariages Mixtes Et Mariages Étrangers Par Nationalité Du Conjoint." *Tableau 22*. Paris: INSEE. www.insee.fr

King, R., and P. Raghuram. 2013. "International Student Migration: Mapping the Field and New Research Agendas." *Population, Space and Place* 19: 127 137. doi:10.1002/psp.1746.

Lambert, M. C. 2002. *Longing for Exile: Migration and the Making of a Translocal Community in Senegal, West Africa*. Portsmouth, NH: Heinemann.

Levinson, B. A., D. E. Foley, and D. C. Holland. 1996. *The Cultural Production of the Educated Person: Critical Ethnographies of Schooling and Local Practice*. Albany: State University of New York Press.

Linares, O. 1992. *Power, Prayer and Production: The Jola of Casamance*. Cambridge: Cambridge University Press.

Manchuelle, F. 1997. *Willing Migrants: Soninke Labor Diasporas, 1848 1960*. Athens: Ohio University Press.

Meillassoux, C. 1981. *Maidens, Meal and Money: Capitalism and the Domestic Economy*. Cambridge: Cambridge University Press.

Neveu Kringelbach, H. 2013. *Dance Circles: Movement, Morality and Self Fashioning in Urban Senegal*. Oxford: Berghahn.

Olwig, K. F. 2007. *Caribbean Journeys: An Ethnography of Migration and Home in Three Family Networks*. Durham, NC: Duke University Press.

Olwig, K. F., and N. N. Sørensen. 2002. "Mobile Livelihoods: Making a Living in the World." In *Mobile Livelihoods: Life and Livelihoods in a Globalizing World*, edited by K. F. Olwig and N. N. Sørensen, 1 19. London: Routledge.

Paivandi, S. 1998. *L'enquête Sur Les Conditions De Vie Des Étudiants À Paris 8. Rapport Pour L'observatoire De La Vie Étudiante*. Paris: Université de Paris 8.

Raghuram, P. 2013. "Theorising the Spaces of Student Migration." *Population, Space and Place* 19: 138 154. doi:10.1002/psp.1747.

Rao, N. 2010. "Migration, Education and Socio Economic Mobility." *Compare: A Journal of Comparative and International Education* 40 (2), 137 145.

Riccio, B. 2001. "From 'Ethnic Group' to 'Transnational Community'? Senegalese Migrants, Ambivalent Experiences, and Multiple Trajectories." *Journal of Ethnic and Migration Studies* 27 (4): 583 599. doi:10.1080/13691830120090395.

Rodríguez García, D. 2006. "Mixed Marriages and Transnational Families in the Intercultural Context: A Case Study of African Spanish Couples in Catalonia." *Journal of Ethnic and Migration Studies* 32: 403 433. 10.1080/13691830600555186.

Rodríguez García, D. 2012. "Considérations Théoricométhodologiques Autour De La Mixité." *Enfances, Familles, Générations* 17: 41 58. doi:10.7202/1013414ar.

Safi, M. 2008. "Intermarriage and Assimilation: Disparities in Levels of Exogamy among Immigrants in France." *Population* 63 (2): 239 268. doi:10.3917/pope.802.0239.

Salomon, C. 2009. "Antiquaires Et Businessmen De La Petite Côte Du Sénégal. Le Commerce Des Illusions Amoureuses." *Cahiers d'Etudes Africaines* 1 2 (193 194): 147 176.

Selly Baro, S. 2005. "Quête du savoir et stratégies d'insertion professionnelle: parcours d'émigration des étudiants et cadres sénégalais en France, aux Etats Unis et au Québec." Unpublished PhD thesis, EHESS.

Song, M. 2009. "Is Intermarriage a Good Indicator of Integration?" *Journal of Ethnic and Migration Studies* 35 (2): 331 348. doi:10.1080/13691830802586476.

Todd, E. 1994. *Le Destin Des Immigrés. Assimilation Et Ségrégation Dans Les Démocraties Occidentales*. Paris: Seuil.

Tribalat, M. 2009. "Mariages 'Mixtes' Et Immigration En France." *Espace, Populations, Sociétés* 2: 203 214.

UNESCO, Institut de Statistiques. 2013. Profil éducation Sénégal.

Vaillant, J. 2006. *Vie De Léopold Sédar Senghor: Noir, Français Et Africain*. Paris: Karthala.

Valentin, K. 2012. "The Role of Education in Mobile Livelihoods: Social and Geographical Routes of Young Nepalese Migrants in India." *Anthropology & Education Quarterly* 43 (4): 429 442. doi:10.1111/j.1548 1492.2012.01195.x.

Waters, J. L. 2006. "Geographies of Cultural Capital: Education, International Migration and Family Strategies between Hong Kong and Canada." *Transactions of the Institute of British Geographers* 31 (2): 179 192. doi:10.1111/j.1475 5661.2006.00202.x.

White, O. 1999. *Children of the French Empire: Miscegenation and Colonial Society in French West Africa, 1895 1960*. Oxford: Oxford University Press.

'La Lenin is my passport': schooling, mobility and belonging in socialist Cuba and its diaspora

Mette Louise Berg

Based on an ethnographic study of transnational networks of alumni of an academically selective boarding school in Havana, this article explores the nexus between mobility, schooling and belonging in the context of socialist Cuba and its diaspora. Drawing on Goffman's work, I argue that the boarding school experience was transformative; it facilitated or consolidated social mobility for its pupils, which later, for many, led to geographic mobility in the form of study and work outside Cuba. After graduating, alumni continue to identify with the school and to reproduce their alumni identities. The affective webs of belonging forged through family links and friendships fostered at the school constitute emotionally sustaining networks that also provide material support after migrating. I propose that the school represents a site of identification for a globally dispersed non national diaspora and argue that migration scholars need to embed international migration within people's lives more broadly.

Formal education has been a central tenet in the quest for modernity and nation-hood across post-colonial societies in the twentieth century. Schools have been harnessed to 'inculcate the skills, subjectivities, and disciplines that undergird the modern nation-state' (Levinson and Holland 1996, 1) with the aim of producing national subjects. Yet education also fosters aspirations of geographic mobility beyond national borders (Czaika and de Haas 2013). In Cuba, this tension has proven challenging for the socialist government. Free education for all was a key principle of the 1959 Cuban Revolution, and was seen as a necessity by the revolutionary leaders if Cuba was to become a modern, independent, socialist state. Educational policy and reform therefore were closely tied to nationalism and the transformation of Cuba into a socialist society. Yet, many of those who were educated within the socialist system have chosen to leave Cuba. Their emigration not only represents a loss of skilled personnel, but also constitutes a political embarrassment for the revolutionary government.

Based on an ethnographic study of the transnational networks of alumni of the V.I. Lenin Vocational School (*La Lenin*), an academically selective boarding school in Havana, this article explores the nexus between schooling, mobility and belonging in the context of socialist Cuba and its diaspora. The mobilities paradigm is helpful in this context for its insistence on paying attention to 'multiple interacting mobilities' (Sheller and Urry 2006, 209) and for the recognition that subjectivities are shaped through movement and relationships to both people and places (Conradson and Mckay 2007, 168; Hage 2005). Specifically, I argue that social and geographic mobilities are intertwined and accordingly need to be conceptualised together: Social mobility through schooling often leads to desires for geographic mobility, while geographic mobility is often pursued or desired in order to facilitate social mobility.

Several scales of intertwining mobilities were important to my research subjects. These ranged from the move from neighbourhood school to the prestigious and nationally recognised Lenin School, and later to university studies, sometimes abroad, but also the move from parental home to boarding school and later international migration. Echoing arguments from literature on rural–urban migration (King and Skeldon 2010), for many of my interlocutors, their initial move from childhood home to boarding school, which was geographically small-scale, carried more significance and was seen as involving a bigger change in their lives than their later transnational mobility. Leaving the family home constituted a moment of growing up and becoming independent. Additionally, becoming a pupil at the school entailed the conferring of substantial social prestige, in some cases signifying the consolidation of elite status and in others upward social mobility. In all cases, the school provided a transformational experience.

Yet the mobilities paradigm does not provide conceptual tools for analysing the importance of migrants' networks and identification with compatriots or co-ethnics, the focus for this article. I therefore also draw on the concept of diaspora. As is increasingly acknowledged by scholars, it is problematic to assume *a priori* that diasporic subjects identify first and foremost with their homeland, that is, as national subjects. Often, relationships to significant others and/or localities such as parental home, neighbourhood, city or region constitute more significant sites of identification to migrants than the nation (Berg 2011; Conradson and Mckay 2007, 169; Olwig 2007). In this case, diasporic alumni of the Lenin School identify strongly with their school. A woman now living in New Jersey stated emphatically: 'the school made me who I am', and a man living in Mallorca called it 'a legacy, like a brotherhood, it marks you'. While not all alumni feel so strongly about the school, for many it is a very significant part of their self-identification suggesting an intimate link between schooling and a sense of self. Identification with the school manifests itself in a plethora of Internet sites dedicated to the school, most prominent of which is www.Lalenin.com, numerous online social networking groups, and a corpus of poetry and music paying homage to the school. Offline, alumni maintain friendships often transnationally, and some participate in regular alumni meetings.

In the politicised context of Cuba's relationship with its diaspora, expressions of identification with the school rather than the nation are particularly significant.

The nationalism of the government like that of the self-defined representatives of '*the* Cuban exile community' (Eckstein 2009) insist on exclusive, territorially bound loyalties. Yet diasporic alumni of socialist Cuba's most prestigious school do not identify with either side. In the relational space of their transnational networks, the erstwhile formidable borders of Cuban territorial nationalism are rendered permeable, and a new type of social formation is emerging, part of a diversifying 'new Cuban diaspora', defined not through antagonism to the Cuban regime characteristic of the 'old Cuban diaspora' but rather through shared memories of schooling.

In this article, I suggest that the affective networks of school-based friendships and family relations – the two are increasingly intertwined as alumni intermarry, and recent graduates often constitute the second generation in their family to attend the school – constitute a transnational web of belonging, produced and reproduced through memories, narratives and embodied performances of alumni identity. I critically examine the importance attributed to international mobility over other kinds of mobility in the lives of diasporans and problematise the relationship between nation/nationalism and diaspora.

The article is based on 45 semi-structured interviews conducted in 2012–2013, ranging in duration from about 20 minutes to several hours. Interviewees ranged in age from 19 to early 50s, evenly split between men and women and included pupils at the school between 1972 and 2010, currently living in Cuba, Spain, the UK, the US and France. In addition to interviews and other social interaction with alumni, I am a regular visitor to and observer of the virtual sociality engendered by the web-site www.lalenin.com, managed by an alumnus based in Berlin.[1]

The article begins by outlining the historical context for the creation of the Lenin School. I then proceed to discuss the school as an example of a total institution and the ways in which diasporic alumni remember school life. Finally, I analyse the dynamics of mobility in the lives of my interlocutors and the ways in which they construct networks of belonging.

Education and the New Man in socialist Cuba

In its period of independence before the revolution (1902–1959), Cuba had relatively high rates of literacy in a Latin American context (76% of the population above 10 years of age in 1953). The country was however marked by enormous inequities in wealth, especially between Havana and the rest of the country, with educational resources extremely unevenly distributed and pervasive corruption in the education system (Breidlid 2007, 620; Lutjens 1997). The upper and middle classes tended to send their children to private schools, many of which were religious. These schools often taught a US curriculum and served explicitly as instruments of Americanisation (Epstein 1987; Pérez 1999).

After the revolution, the government nationalised all schools, made primary education free and universal, reorganised secondary and higher education, and initiated its extraordinary literacy campaign with the aim of extending literacy to all Cubans across the country (Leiner 1984; Read 1970; Álvarez Figueroa 1997).[2] Illustrative of the modernist zeal of the revolution and the desire to break with the legacy of private, religious education, schools were to prioritise the sciences and technical skills. Many were located in the countryside, where pupils would spend half the day studying, the other half doing agricultural work, emphasising austerity, discipline and obedience (Smith and Padula 1996, 83).

While it is a common trait of modern schools that children are removed from their families (Levinson and Holland 1996, 1), in revolutionary Cuba this has been more radical than in many other countries. Schools explicitly aimed to minimise the perceived pernicious influence of tradition in families and to discourage 'individualism' (Smith and Padula 1996): The new Cubans were truly to be the children of the revolution. The *Hombre Nuevo*, or New Man, who would be forged in these schools was a man who would sacrifice his personal life for the revolution; he would be co-operative, hardworking, morally pure and disinterested in personal gain; in Ernesto 'Che' Guevara's words, he would be 'unsullied' by the 'original sin of capitalism' (1977, 14).[3]

In this context of a profound restructuring of the educational system to serve new societal needs, the V.I. Lenin School was founded in Havana in 1972. As the name suggests, it was modelled on the Soviet education system, but also inspired by Maoism and the Cuban nationalist hero José Martí's ideals of breaking down the barriers between manual and intellectual labour (Cheng and Manning 2003; Read 1970). La Lenin was meant to be a 'new kind of school', which would, in Castro's words, serve as a 'vanguard' for other schools in a future socialist Cuba (see Wald 1978, 361; Granma 1974, 5), and similar elite schools were opened in Cuba's other provinces. Only the most gifted students from Havana Province were admitted, and if a pupil's marks fell below a certain threshold, they were expelled. In the first years, La Lenin admitted up to 4500 children from the age of 11 until 18; the age range was later changed to 16–18.

The school compound on the outskirts of Havana occupies 66 acres of land, and includes purpose-built accommodation and teaching facilities, a library, sports fields, Olympic-sized swimming pools, theatres, 45 fully equipped language and science labs, an infirmary, hairdressers and a factory where the pupils were to work part-time.[4] The considerable investment that these facilities represent, testify to the significance the school had for the revolutionary government. In the words of one alumnus whose father had been among the first cohorts, it was 'the dream of the revolution at that time'. The school's special status was marked by frequent visits by the revolution's highest leaders and international dignitaries.

In the absence of access to the official school records, it is difficult to establish the socio-economic profile of pupils and how it has changed over the years. In terms of gender, women were in the majority at elite schools across the country by the late 1980s (Lutjens 1997, 295). At the national level, there has been an increasing feminisation of further and higher studies from the 1980s onwards, reflecting women's higher grade attainments and the competitive entry requirements of Cuba's universities (Domínguez García 1999, 136–137). From interviews and testimonies of alumni it is evident that the vast majority of pupils at the school historically and at present are 'white' [*blanca/o*], reflecting long-standing problems of racialised inequality and structural racism in Cuba (Fernandez 2010).

In terms of class profile, many children of the revolutionary elite studied at the school. While I have not interviewed any offspring of the top leaders, one interlocutor was the son of a vice-minister, and several others were sons and daughters of high-ranking government officials. The quota system of allocating a set number of places to all municipalities in Havana Province suggests that academically able children from poor neighbourhoods have a chance of entering, and some interviews, especially with alumni from the first two decades, confirm this. A man now living in New Jersey remembered of his time in the school:

> There were definitely people from poorer backgrounds and from the middle classes, but the people from the upper class never missed [being admitted]. ... I entered in ... 1972 ... The children of Fidel [Castro] studied in my year, three of them; Che [Guevara's] daughter ... the children of all the ministers [and] important personalities ... Between all of these were the rest of us who didn't come from powerful families.

The overall sample of interviewees suggests that children from families with substantial cultural capital are over-represented. Many alumni of more recent cohorts took private classes to pass the entry exams. That their families were able and prepared to spend hard currency on private tuition to ensure their children's entry into the school is indicative of the enduring prestige of the school as well as of the class profile of its pupils. When asked if he would define La Lenin as an elite school, Andris, who was at the school in the mid-1990s, quickly said, 'yes, it's an elite school *par excellence*'. He continued:

> Of course the 2000 [students at the school when he studied] were not all of the elite, *but* there were many, many sons and daughters of government ministers ... I don't think that they favour them as such, but it's because they're the ones who were able to pay a private teacher to help them study. These children only had to worry about studying, they didn't have to do other things, they didn't have to worry about how to put food on the table ... So, it's an elite school in all meanings of the term.

Yet not all families were keen for their children to go to the school and some saw the school as a threat to family unity and patriarchal control, especially in the first two decades of the school's existence. Clara, who now lives in Miami, recounted strong family opposition in the late 1970s:

> I entered La Lenin against the will of my family. I was an only child, raised by my grandparents because my parents had divorced. Nobody in my family had any education; they had left school after 3rd or 6th grade. ... we were *guajiros*

[peasants]. But I did well in school … and I knew I wanted to try to go to La Lenin so I sat the exam without telling my grandfather. When the letter arrived to say I had been accepted they didn't want me to go at first, but I pleaded with them and said 'don't do this to me, please, it is the best school, I want to go to university'. They … were worried that I would have sexual relations, pick up bad language and that I would have relations with blacks yes, I'm ashamed to say so, but my grandfather was very racist! I pleaded with them and in the end they said I could go, but if I came back speaking bad language or if I changed from what I was, they would take me out immediately. I didn't change! I kept saying 'may I', 'thank you', 'please' and so on at home, I never used bad language.

By contrast, recent graduates describe family support for them to enter the school, reflecting the growing recognition over time that the school offers the best education available in the country. It is also significant that many parents later on were themselves alumni who wanted their children to have the same opportunities that they had:

Claudia (studied at the school in the late 1990s, now lives in Spain): From I was born, I was surrounded by people from La Lenin because my father's best friends were from La Lenin, or rather, they *are* from La Lenin and according to him, the best years of his life were in La Lenin, well, that's what we all say … I always aspired to go to La Lenin … It was completely clear to me that my first priority was La Lenin.

Maria (studied at the school in the late 1990s, older brother also studied there, father studied at predecessor school, now lives in Spain): It was an objective that was so clear to me that I took it for granted that I would get in … In fact, it wasn't difficult for me. I mean, I *knew* I was going to be at La Lenin, it was a certainty that not everyone has.

In the first years, pupils whose families were supportive of the revolution and who themselves showed political commitment to it, were favoured for entry, but the opposite was also sometimes the case. A woman who studied at the school in its early years believed she had been admitted to provoke her father who was then a political prisoner. She described the school as 'a brainwash' (because of its ideological indoctrination) but equally as 'a blessing' (because of its high level of education) and remained proud of being an alumnus, referring to the broad education she had received, the many things she had learnt including from the manual labour and the superior facilities of the school. After graduating, she had a distinguished career in Cuba, but later migrated to the US to join her father who had left Cuba after completing his prison term.

La Lenin as a total institution

The hold that La Lenin continues to exert over its alumni even after they graduate needs to be understood as a function of the kind of institution it is. The school is an example of what Erving Goffman has defined as a 'total institution', that is 'a place of residence and work where a large number of like-situated individuals, cut off from the wider society for an appreciable period of time, together lead an enclosed formally administered round of life' (1968, 11). Goffman's analysis, based on his covert research at a psychiatric hospital in Washington, DC, in the 1950s, proved a powerful critique of psychiatric hospitals at the time, and the concept of the total institution has been helpfully applied in other contexts since then (Scott 2010; Davies 1989). Goffman's insight that in a total institution, the self can usefully be seen not as 'a property of the person to whom it is attributed', but rather as *constituted* through the prevailing institutional arrangements (1968, 154), is especially helpful for understanding the degree of identification between La Lenin and its alumni.

The learning and inculcation of body techniques (Mauss 1979) is an important aspect of this constitution of the self. Pupils' bodily dispositions were moulded and disciplined through repetitive daily routines, such as the making up of beds followed by inspection every morning. One man explained to me how he still makes up his bed in the exact way that he learnt at La Lenin more than 30 years after graduating, and it was a source of regret to him that his adult sons did not follow his example. Members of early cohorts remember the rhythmic school applause, used during assemblies and meetings, and now reproduced at alumni meetings. More recent graduates assert that they can spot fellow *leninistas* by their distinctive speech and manner of dancing. Remembering La Lenin and being a *leninista* or someone from La Lenin thus encompasses both narrative and embodied memories that are mobilised, performed and reproduced when alumni meet, and which set them apart from contemporaries who did not go to the school.

Goffman describes five 'rough groupings' of total institutions (1968, 16), and defines boarding schools as belonging within a group of institutions 'purportedly established the better to pursue some worklike task and justifying themselves only on these instrumental grounds' (1968, 16). Overall, he saw total institutions as coercive and degrading to inmates, allowing them only very restricted agency (see Scott [2010] for critique). This assessment is sharply at odds with the enthusiastic and positive accounts of life at La Lenin in my interviews. The contrast requires an acknowledgement of the qualitative differences between a prestigious institution like La Lenin and other types of institutions with which Goffman lumps boarding schools (see also Davies 1989, 82–83).

Christie Davies's alternative classification of total institutions according to their purpose, degree of openness or closure and mode of compliance, is more helpful. In her scheme, boarding schools emerge as an intermediate total institution in terms of relative openness, and as characterised by normative control and the aim of transmogrification of its inmates rather than internment as an end in itself (1989, 90). For while none of my interlocutors explicitly made this point, becoming a pupil at the school entailed a degree of rendering oneself to the revolutionary project, and submitting to a process of social, educational and political transmogrification. To illustrate, pupils were expected to participate in events in support of the government such as May Day marches. At times of heightened political mobilisation, the demand on pupils' time could be considerable. During the Mariel boatlift in 1980 or the Elián González affair in 2000, pupils missed a substantial number of classes as they were taken in school buses to participate in demonstrations. In the words of one interlocutor, pupils at La Lenin were always 'Fidel's first column'. Some families were adverse to this political indoctrination. The alumni themselves saw it as at most a small sacrifice in light of the superior education they received. Clara, whose grandfather did not want her to go to La Lenin, was pragmatic:

> I didn't want to lose out on the language lab, the chemistry lab, the three swimming pools and so on, so of course I went. My grandparents resented that I was being used for political stuff.

Notwithstanding, participating in protest marches did not necessarily have much of an impact on pupils' political consciousness; several commented that they primarily remembered the marches as welcome breaks from the school routine.

In a recent extension of Goffman's work, Susie Scott discusses 'academic hothouses' as examples of what she calls 'reinventive institutions'. These are late twentieth century versions of total institutions, defined as 'places to which people retreat for periods of intense self-reflection, education, enrichment and reform, but under their own volition, in pursuit of "self-improvement"' (2010, 218). In reinventive institutions, peer relations characterised by 'emotional intensity' and a 'culture of commitment' are of crucial importance (2010, 225). Scott's descriptive register resonates better with the many accounts of intense, supportive friendships and deeply felt commitment, than Goffman's account of degradation and lack of strong peer bonds.

Iván: Whenever I see [my friends from La Lenin] it makes me really happy, we always talk and joke, it's as if time hadn't passed at all … it's like we were still room-mates. … We met 17 years ago and we know each other so well that it's as if we've known each other all of our lives.

The mutual support is well illustrated in the numerous accounts of food sharing. In the first decade, the school provided abundant food to its pupils, but alumni from later periods remember food scarcity, reflecting the wider problems of food provisioning in Cuba, especially during the so-called 'Special Period' of severe economic crisis in Cuba following the disappearance of the Socialist Bloc (Eckstein 2003). Memories of sharing food brought from home with room-mates therefore carry strong emotional significance:

Claudia (studied at the school in the late 1990s, now lives in Spain): We got on very well with each other, we were very close. There was one of the other girls who always brought a tin of sardines in tomato sauce [from home] ... we were eight room-mates and all eight of us ate from the tin. She always religiously divided the sardines between the eight of us.

Such accounts were often accompanied by assertions to the effect that the school was 'marvellous', 'wonderful', 'a paradise', whether the interlocutor graduated decades or merely a few years ago. A woman who was a pupil at the Lenin School in the mid-1980s, before training as a medic, and who now lives in New Jersey, said: 'it was the best thing that happened to me'; 'the school was my home, my family, everything'. This positive assertion of a self, moulded by and in the school, is far removed from the 'amoral arts of shamelessness' as the end point of the 'moral career' of the mental patient described by Goffman (1968, 155).

Life at La Lenin remembered

Memories are not 'simply records of the past', they are 'interpretive reconstructions', embedded in particular cultural and social contexts of recall and commemoration (Antze and Lambek 1996, vii). Analysing memory narratives therefore provides insight into the tensions and disjunctures between the intentions of La Lenin and the state for its children and young people and what they themselves make of it, something which is missing in many accounts of education, including in Cuba (see also Froerer [2007], Charon-Cardona [2013], Domínguez García and Lutjens [2002]).

The accounts of life at La Lenin by alumni are surprisingly consistent despite the up to 40 years separating their time at the school. They describe a daily life entirely contained within the school compound, consisting of strictly regimented days starting with wake-up calls on the central tannoy at 6am, followed by morning exercises, inspection, breakfast and classes. Most students were required to participate in manual labour either in the fields, the on-site factory, or to clean the school, two–three afternoons every week. High-performing students were selected for extra classes and were generally exempt from manual labour. The evenings were dedicated to independent study with one evening a week set aside for entertainment organised by the school. Pupils would usually go home every weekend, although this right might be taken away as punishment for disciplinary infringements.

Some alumni describe the school as run with 'military discipline', with penalty points added to report cards for minor infringements. This is how Iván, who studied at the school in the mid-1990s, and who now lives in Spain, recalled disciplinary enforcement:

The thing about discipline was very important ... Men weren't allowed earrings, it was firmly prohibited, always short hair, and you had to wear the uniform correctly. The monogram had to be exactly halfway down the sleeve ... Trousers had to have straight legs, they couldn't be tight ... I've ... had reports for long hair and once I had to stay behind for one day during the weekend to do little jobs in the garden.

There is little evidence of an extensive or organised 'underlife' at La Lenin. Most likely this is explained by the high degree of normative solidarity between pupils, and between pupils and the school (Davies 1989, 93). There are some hints in stories of subversion of the school dress code, including also unauthorised escapes, and other similar small-scale acts of resistance (Scott 1986). Some interviewees did mention negative memories of the school. These include one man who disliked the discipline at the school and being away from his family so much that he decided to leave; another man who retrospectively identified himself as a bully and who felt shameful about his past behaviour; and one man who said he had no memory whatever of his time at the school, suggesting it had not been unambiguously happy. However, I have not heard a single alumnus dismiss their education. A woman in her early thirties, now living in Paris, commented that none of the students in her year group would be capable of criticising 'the system' because it is 'good'. Equally, very few recount examples of abuses of power, bullying or ritual humiliation, which are such staples of accounts of elite boarding schools, for example in Britain. What stands out is rather a strong, positive feeling of belonging to the school and its community of students. For some La Lenin additionally provided an escape from dysfunctional family homes.

In the early years of the school's existence dormitories were large, but this was later changed to smaller, eight-pupil cubicles. The small group of room-mates became a sort of substitute family with whom pupils shared daily life.

Iván: It's wonderful because you arrive at the school at a conflictive age, but you have to reach a point where you know people. The first time you shower you see everyone naked so you end up knowing people completely. ... It is also the age of discovering your sexuality and you simply can't imagine the conversations we had in the dormitories at night, from advice to absolutely everything, everything is told. Some people are more timid, some people less. People would say things like 'I have a girlfriend and I don't know what to do, she is more experienced than me' or the opposite case 'she is like a little girl, what can I do?'

Alumni also have fond memories of the academic rigour of the school and its dedicated teachers. Many Lenin alumni have later taught others and often mention teachers at La Lenin as their role model.

Andris: I had been used to being number one in my secondary school. I had the best grades ... without having to study much because the level wasn't very high. ... At La Lenin it was serious, you really had to study because if you didn't, you wouldn't qualify [to stay at the school].

And of course you knew that it wasn't enough just to pass ... it was about getting the best marks.

Pupils at La Lenin regularly won national and international competitions in maths, chemistry and physics. The level was such that for some the first years at university were merely repeating what they had already learnt at the school. One woman who had to leave the school for not achieving high enough grades, subsequently found herself top of her class in her local high school. Surprisingly given the many accounts of a highly competitive atmosphere where everyone was ranked against each other, I have heard no accounts of resentment among pupils. By contrast, after graduating, and especially during their years at university, some Lenin alumni commented that other students who did not go to La Lenin resented their identification with the school and their perceived air of superiority.

Because the vast majority of Lenin alumni go on to study within the fields of science, engineering or architecture they are often well placed to help each other. And because their children also go to the school, the web of connections and the scope for support has widened and deepened over time to cover not just the world of work. As an example, Beatriz, a woman in her fifties living in Havana, was a pupil at the school in the 1970s; several of her close relatives also went. She married a schoolmate with whom she had two children who both went to the school. After divorcing, Beatriz married another alumnus. These relations of kin, friends and marriage make up a dense web against which Beatriz's life unfolds. When she moved to a new neighbourhood, a fellow alumnus introduced her and her husband to their new neighbours, and she also secured her current job thanks to her alumni network. When alumni leave Cuba, this same web of affective relationships and material support extends transnationally with alumni staying in touch like other transnational migrants do (Vertovec 2009) and helping each other in the new country.

Claudia: The experience I've had here [in Spain] is that people [i.e. other alumni] recognise that you're from La Lenin and you end up with a closer relationship ... it makes you relate a little more ... It's like a point of reference ... it helps you ... especially in terms of work.

Sometimes, transnational mobility itself is facilitated with the help of other alumni. To illustrate, Andris left Cuba with a scholarship to study at a Spanish university. A friend from La Lenin who was already living in Spain helped him during the application process and when he arrived his friends from La Lenin picked him up at the airport:

[My friends] are almost all from La Lenin ... some of them are friends from university but they also went to La Lenin ... They organised a party for me when I arrived. It was more like moving from one neighbourhood to the next, I was already well integrated when I arrived here. ... I really enjoy living here ... I miss my parents, but I don't really miss Cuba. Basically what one misses isn't that bit of land anyway, it's the people and they're not there anyway ... my generation are all outside of Cuba.

The scope for mutual support is greater where Lenin alumni are residentially clustered, principally in the US, Miami especially, and in Barcelona and Madrid in Spain. Gladys was at the school in the early 1980s, and is married to another alumnus. She works at a public university in Miami where she often meets Lenin alumni among the students. She said she spots them from their manner of speaking and that, when she can, she helps them find jobs through other alumni who are running businesses in the Miami area. Iván had the same experience in Spain:

> I maintain [my friendships from La Lenin] ... from my class at La Lenin ... six of us graduated together in the same year from the University [of Havana]. We spent 5 years together at university as well [as the 3 years at La Lenin]. ... Alexis lives in Barcelona and we stay in touch a lot. ... He's reached a good position and he's always offering me jobs.

Conclusion: La Lenin transnational

The title of this article 'La Lenin is my passport' is a quote from an interview with Claudia who now lives in Spain. Being an alumna of La Lenin is a vital aspect of her self-identification, to the extent that she claims it as her homeland: 'I say frankly that I am from La Lenin'. It resonates with similar assertions by other alumni, who, like her, live outside Cuba. This suggests a paradox: The Cuban government founded La Lenin to produce political subjects who would serve and govern socialist Cuba. By definition, if the school was successful, its alumni would therefore stay. Yet, as Levinson and Holland have noted, schools have often proven themselves a 'contradictory resource for those who would fit the young to a particular version of society' (1996, 1).

The material I have presented shows that the school was successful in the sense that alumni remain deeply committed to the institution that proved so decisive in shaping their lives. They are grateful for the education they received and appreciative of the opportunities it bestowed upon them, *but* many of them now live in diaspora. The paradox is best explained, I suggest, by paying close attention to the intertwining of social and geographic mobilities and to the texture of everyday life at the school. The school became a transformational experience which set its pupils on a path of what Ghassan Hage (2005) calls 'existential mobility'. This is the kind of mobility which makes people feel they are 'going somewhere' in their lives. Hage argues that it is when people do not have a sense of existential mobility, that they start contemplating physical mobility. In this case, the horizons widened and the friendships forged at school proved decisive for many alumni and fostered a feeling of exactly this kind of existential mobility. Alumni almost all explained their emigration from Cuba in terms of aspirations for existential mobility, in the form of careers and an overall sense of better opportunities in life. Their physical mobility out of Cuba was, in turn, supported and facilitated by the strong social networks of support fostered at the school, as well as the cultural and educational capital it bestowed. As Andris described it, moving to Spain was like 'moving from one neighbourhood to the next'. For him, as for others, the big, existential move was *geographically* small scale, from their local school to La Lenin.

My material further shows that schools can become sites for non-national affiliation and identification, raising wider questions about belonging and diaspora formation in a context of globalisation and transnational migration of elites and the highly skilled. While none of my interlocutors explicitly made the point, identification with the school provides a highly ambiguous identity narrative, an alternative to the polarising discourse and counter-discourse of the government and organised Cuban exile organisations, respectively. The appeal of this alternative narrative further underlines the importance of taking into account the pre-migration experiences of diasporans, completely overlooked in assimilationist literature, which is otherwise keenly interested in the educational achievements of migrants. It also points to the need to embed international migration within people's lives more broadly and not presume *a priori* that mobility across national borders is more important than other kinds of mobility.

Acknowledgements

I am grateful to interviewees for their time, to Margalida Mulet Pascual for research assistance, to Vanessa Ramos Castillo for transcriptions and to the John Fell Fund for funding. Thank you also to the guest editors and two anonymous peer reviewers for their insightful and constructive comments.

Notes

1. Interviewees were recruited using a snowball approach, drawing on existing contacts from prior research. Margalida Mulet Pascual conducted some interviews for me, recruited via her own contacts. All interviews were conducted in Spanish. Names and some details of interviewees have been changed to protect their anonymity.
2. For a review of scholarship on education in revolutionary Cuba, see Lutjens (1998).
3. On the gender implications of the idea of the New Man, see Behar (2000).
4. Not all these facilities are in use today.

References

Álvarez Figueroa, O. 1997. "El Sistema Educativo Cubano En Los Noventa." *Papers. Revista De Sociología* 52: 115 137.

Antze, P., and M. Lambek. 1996. "Preface." In *Tense Past. Cultural Essays in Trauma and Memory*, edited by P. Antze and M. Lambek, vii ix. New York: Routledge.

Behar, R. 2000. "Post Utopia: the Erotics of Power and Cuba's Revolutionary Children." In *Cuba, the Elusive Nation. Interpretations of National Identity*, edited by D. J. Fernández and M. C. Betancourt, 134 154. Gainesville: University Press of Florida.

Berg, M. L. 2011. *Diasporic Generations: Memory, Politics, and Nation among Cubans in Spain*. Oxford: Berghahn Books.

Breidlid, A. 2007. "Education in Cuba an Alternative Educational Discourse: Lessons to be Learned?" *Compare: A Journal of Comparative and International Education* 37 (5): 617 634.

Charon Cardona, E. 2013. "Socialism and Education in Cuba and Soviet Uzbekistan." *Globalisation, Societies and Education* 11 (2): 296 313. doi:10.1080/14767724.2013.782204.

Cheng, Y., and P. Manning. 2003. "Revolution in Education: China and Cuba in Global Context, 1957 76." *Journal of World History* 14 (3): 359 391. doi:10.1353/jwh.2003.0031.

Conradson, D., and D. Mckay. 2007. "Translocal Subjectivities: Mobility, Connection, Emotion." *Mobilities* 2 (2): 167 174. doi:10.1080/17450100701381524.

Czaika, M., and H. de Haas. 2013. The Globalisation of Migration: Has the World Really Become More Migratory? *International Migration Institute Working Papers*, Vol. 68. Oxford: University of Oxford.

Davies, C. 1989. "Goffman's Concept of the Total Institution: Criticisms and Revisions." *Human Studies* 12: 77 95. doi:10.1007/BF00142840.

Domínguez García, M. I. 1999. "Acceso a La Educación Y Cuestiones De Género En Cuba." *Revista Bimestre Cubano* 11: 131 144.

Domínguez García, M. I., and S. L. Lutjens. 2002. "La Participación En Las Escuelas Cubanas: La Federación De Estudiantes De La Enseñanza Media (FEEM)". Comparative and International Education Society annual conference. Orlando, FL.

Eckstein, S. 2003. *Back from the Future. Cuba under Castro*. London: Routledge.

Eckstein, S. 2009. *The Immigrant Divide: How Cuban Americans Changed the US and their Homeland*. London: Routledge.

Epstein, E. H. 1987. "The Peril of Paternalism: the Imposition of Education on Cuba by the United States." *American Journal of Education* 96 (1): 1 23. doi:10.1086/443879.

Fernandez, N. T. 2010. *Revolutionizing Romance: Interracial Couples in Contemporary Cuba*. New Brunswick: Rutgers University Press.

Froerer, P. 2007. "Disciplining the Saffron Way: Moral Education and the Hindu Rashtra." *Modern Asian Studies* 41 (5): 1033 1071. doi:10.1017/S0026749X06002587.

Goffman, E. 1968. *Asylums: Essays on the Social Situation of Mental Patients and Other Inmates*. Harmondsworth: Penguin Books.

Granma. 1974. "Una Escuela Donde Se Forman Hombres". Un taller donde se forjan comunistas. Granma. pp. 1 6, February.

Guevara, E. C. 1977. *El Socialismo Y El Hombre Nuevo*. Mexico City: Siglo Veintiuno Editores sa.

Hage, G. 2005. "A Not so Multi Sited Ethnography of A Not so Imagined Community." *Anthropological Theory* 5 (4): 463 475. doi:10.1177/1463499605059232.

King, R. and R. Skeldon. 2010. "'Mind the Gap!' Integrating Approaches to Internal and International Migration." *Journal of Ethnic and Migration Studies* 36 (10): 1619 1646. doi:10.1080/1369183X.2010.489380.

Leiner, M. 1984. "Cuba's Schools: 25 Years Later." In *Cuba: Twenty Five Years of Revolution, 1959 1984*, edited by S. Halebsky and J. M. Kirk, 27 44. New York: Praeger.

Levinson, B. A., and D. C. Holland. 1996. "The Cultural Production of the Educated Person: An Introduction." In *The Cultural Production of the Educated Person*, edited by B. A. Levinson, D. E. Foley, and D. C. Holland, 1 54. Albany: State University of New York Press.

Lutjens, S. L. 1997. "Women, Education, and the State in Cuba." In *Latin American Education: Comparative Perspectives*, edited by C. A. Torres and A. Puiggrós, 289 319. Boulder, CO: Westview Press.

Lutjens, S. L. 1998. "Education and the Cuban Revolution: A Selected Bibliography." *Comparative Education Review* 42 (2): 197 224.

Mauss, M. 1979. "The Notion of Body Techniques." In *Sociology and Psychology: Essays*, 97 105, London: Routledge & Kegan Paul.

Olwig, K. F. 2007. *Caribbean Journeys: An Ethnography of Migration and Home in Three Family Networks*. Durham, NC: Duke University Press.

Pérez, L. A. 1999. *On Becoming Cuban: Identity, Nationality, and Culture*. Chapel Hill: University of North Carolina Press.

Read, G. H. 1970. "The Cuban Revolutionary Offensive in Education." *Comparative Education Review* 14 (2): 131 143. doi:10.1086/445463.

Scott, J. 1986. "Everyday Forms of Peasant Resistance." *Journal of Peasant Studies* 13 (2): 5 35. doi:10.1080/03066158608438289.

Scott, S. 2010. "Revisiting the Total Institution: Performative Regulation in the Reinventive Institution." *Sociology* 44 (2): 213 231. doi:10.1177/0038038509357198.

Sheller, M., and J. Urry. 2006. "The New Mobilities Paradigm." *Environment and Planning A* 38 (2): 207 226. doi:10.1068/a37268.

Smith, L. M., and A. Padula. 1996. *Sex and Revolution: Women in Socialist Cuba*. New York: Oxford University Press.

Vertovec, S. 2009. *Transnationalism*. London: Routledge.

Wald, K. 1978. *Children of Che: Childcare and Education in Cuba*. Palo Alto, CA: Ramparts Press.

Transnational education and the remaking of social identity: Nepalese student migration to Denmark

Karen Valentin

There is no significant history of migration from Nepal to Denmark, but the post conflict situation in Nepal and the expansion of an international, com mercialised education market have resulted in a significant number of Nepalese students in Denmark. This article argues, first, that the current forms of student migration from Nepal must be examined within the context of broader class based mobility practices and the consolidation of a relatively new middle class in Nepal. Second, it examines the significance of education and educated status for people's claims to belong to the middle class in a transnational context where social status is at stake.

Educational migration, when compared to other forms of migration, offers an excellent vantage point from which to explore individual and collective expectations of social and geographical mobility, because of the strong in-built future orientations of both education and migration. The expanding international education market, which has turned international education into a global mass phenomenon, holds out promises for young people from the emerging middle-classes in countries of the global South, both as a means of enhancing one's social standing and as a pathway to personal growth and transformation. Contemporary forms of student migration are embedded in historically distinct social and cultural frameworks and must therefore be examined within the context of broader practices of mobility, which condition and shape different people's social and geographical horizons.

With a focus on the production of a middle-class identity in the context of student migration from Nepal to Denmark, this article examines how class-based identities associated with educational achievement are being reinterpreted in processes of transnational mobility. A few scholars have focused on student migration from the global South to the global North, linking it to issues of social stratification (Biao and Shen 2009) and showing how it, embedded within structural global inequalities, in effect becomes an avenue for low-skilled labour migration for young people in blurred zones between legality and illegality (e.g. Baas 2007; Pan 2011; Neilson 2009). In highlighting the overlapping spheres of education and labour in migration processes, these studies emphasise the industrial, and sometimes exploitative, character of organised student migration, but pay less attention to the meanings that migrants and those left behind ascribe to education as one possible long-term livelihood strategy. Furthermore, they tend to ignore the ways in which a student identity can be instrumental in laying claim to and negotiating middle-class status. This article recognises the fundamentally uneven structures that govern contemporary forms of international student mobility (Brooks and Waters 2011), but it argues against common understandings of migration as linear movements of either upward or downward social mobility by addressing the way in which migrants actively work on reclaiming a social status to which they feel themselves entitled, even in situations of temporarily experienced downwards social mobility.

The fact that migrants are embedded within, and differentiated, by class relations and that this in itself contributes to producing mobility and immobility (Lem and Barber 2010, 3–4) is central for understanding not just who migrates where and under what conditions, but also the positions available to different categories of mobile people within and across different locations. By approaching class as a process and as a cultural project that is constantly in the making (Liechty 2003; Dickey 2012), the article takes its point of departure in middle-class perspectives. What characterises 'middle-class-ness' is not just access to economic resources, but equally the way in which it is performed with the aim of claiming a social identity distinct from both those above and those below oneself in the class hierarchy (Liechty 2003; Dickey 2012). A middle-class perspective is illuminating in order to comprehend both the demands for social recognition and the vulnerability of certain categories of migrants, who see themselves as relatively privileged and mobile in some contexts, but whose social status may become less secure in transnational contexts.

Focusing on Nepalese youths' motivations for pursuing higher education in Denmark, this article examines how current practices of student migration are linked to the consolidation of a relatively new middle-class in Nepal. Until 2006, Nepal was officially a Hindu kingdom and access to formal education has historically been restricted by privileges linked to the caste system and by concomitant ideas of ritual purity and impurity (Valentin 2005). During the second half of the twentieth century, competing status hierarchies based on socio-economic standing became manifest, *inter alia*, in a distinctly urban and highly consumer-oriented middle-class whose status partly depended on their ability to purchase access to education (Liechty 2003). This demand for private education led to an explosion in the number of private educational institutions and, by implication, the development of a two-tier education system consisting of underfunded, state-run schools and a wide range of private schools of varying quality and price (Valentin 2005). In recent years, this marketisation of education has been rendered visible by the vast numbers of educational consultancies operating in Nepal, all competing to attract prospective students for study abroad.

The existing scholarly literature on Nepalese transnational migration mostly focuses on low-skilled labour migration to India, the Middle East and Far East, portraying it as an economic survival strategy for poor households (e.g. Kollmair et al. 2006; Seddon, Adhikari, and Gurung 2002; Thieme and Müller-Böker 2004). Despite the increasing number of Nepalese migrating with the purpose of obtaining a degree from abroad, the issue of student migration has only been addressed marginally, either in economic terms as 'brain gain/drain' (Bhattarai 2011) or as secondary to discussions of professional nurse migration to the UK (Adhikari 2009/10) and transnational networks among Nepalese migrants, including students, in the US (Sijapati 2009/10). While these studies focus on dimensions of migration – the marketisation of international labour and education markets as well as the social organisation of migrant communities – that are certainly relevant to Nepalese students in Denmark, the issue of mobility is less developed. This article argues that migration is an integrated practice of many Nepalese households (Sharma 2008), and that contemporary forms of student migration must be examined in relation to existing practices of geographical mobility. Shedding light on the relationship between education and the formation of class-based identities in transnational migration, I deliberately foreground a perspective on class to one on caste, partly because caste does not figure as a prominent theme in the empirical data, and partly because of the role ascribed to formal education in middle-class formation in South Asia in general (Fernandes 2011). For most Nepalese, an education abroad is a middle-class privilege, but because class positions are dynamic and fundamentally unstable (Dickey 2012), a position in the 'middle' cannot be taken for granted. Instead, I argue, it must be actively maintained by migrants, especially in situations where social status is at stake. This is the case for the many Nepalese who are forced to engage in low-skilled manual labour while studying in Denmark in order to earn a living and who are consistently portrayed in the Danish media as potential 'immigrants' who are just using their student visa as an entry to the labour market.

The article is based on ethnographic data collected among Nepalese migrants in Copenhagen, Denmark, from 2010 to 2013.[1] It consists of in-depth interviews with students, participant observation in social and political events organised by Nepalese migrant organisations, home visits and informal interaction with students, spouses and job-seekers. Seeking to capture the Nepalese students' experiences of the Danish education system and how they as a social category are perceived by other actors within the education system, I interviewed international coordinators, had informal conversations with teachers and participated in classes at a business college. Additional data are drawn from recurrent short visits to Nepal, where I have met returnee student migrants, relatives of current student migrants in Denmark and official stakeholders. The findings are further informed by a long-standing ethnographic interest in educational practices among urban poor in Nepal (Valentin 2005) and the role of formal and informal learning in Nepal-India migration (Valentin 2012a).

Educational migration from Nepal to Denmark

The case of Nepalese students is particularly interesting for exploring the relationship between educational and geographical trajectories because they come from a country which was never colonised and did not therefore develop established pathways for educational migration to the West. India was and still is the principal destination for Nepalese going abroad for both employment and education, but patterns of international migration from Nepal have changed drastically over the last two decades in terms of destinations (see, e.g. Bruslé 2009/10). Prior to the introduction of democracy in 1990, travel to countries other than India was restricted for ordinary people (Gurung and Adhikhari 2004). The relaxation of emigration rules combined with 10 years of armed conflict between government forces and Maoist insurgents (1996–2006) and the ensuing post-conflict situation characterised by political instability contributed to increase emigration from Nepal. Weak state institutions, including the educational system, general lack of occupational opportunities and, during the years of conflict, fear of being conscripted into the armed forces on either side led wealthy families to send their children abroad for education while large numbers of young people from less affluent families left the country in search of salaried work. Broadly speaking, people today tend to migrate to the Middle East and Far East Asia for manual labour, while North America, Australia and Europe have provided pathways for student and highly skilled labour migration for people from the middle and upper classes.

Until the early 2000s, there were few Nepalese in Denmark: a few established families, people who had married Danes, and professionals on temporary training or post-graduate programmes. From around 2003, students began to find their way to Denmark and by the mid-2000s Danish educational institutions, especially business colleges, started to recruit Nepalese students, partly through agents in Nepal. Initially, higher education for foreigners was free of charge in Denmark, but from 2006 fees were introduced for students coming from outside the European Union/European Economic Area (EU/EEA). The Nepalese continued, however, to come to Denmark to enrol in educational programmes, especially the 2-year Academy Profession Programmes at business colleges or 3½-year Professional Bachelor's Programmes at the so-called University Colleges within fields like business management, multimedia design, service and hospitality, and nutrition. Aside from those lucky few who manage to get a scholarship directly from the colleges, students have to pay approximately 20,000 Euro for a 1½–2 years programme, or sometimes more depending upon academic level. After completion, some leave for other European countries, others return to Nepal, and still others stay in Denmark, progressing to Bachelor and Master programmes and using their education as a stepping stone for seeking a Danish Green Card: a scheme for highly educated foreigners who are granted 3 years' residence and a work permit in Denmark for job-seeking purposes.

In Denmark, Nepalese are the third largest group of foreign students from outside Europe; their numbers peaked in 2008, when 710 student visas were issued to Nepalese nationals (Udlændingeservice 2009), but this figure had dropped to 387 in 2012 (Udlændingestyrelsen 2013). According to the students themselves, this decline is the result of restrictive immigration laws and the global economic crisis, which has led to a lack of low-skilled jobs in Denmark, which students rely heavily on in order to earn their living during studies (cf. infra). In the meantime, the number of Green Card holders coming directly from Nepal, spouses (mostly women) and younger children has increased and according to official figures the current number of Nepalese in Denmark is 1951.[2]

Expanding horizons, new destinations

Current forms of transnational student migration must, I contend, be viewed as geographical extensions of pre-existing mobility practices in Nepal, where migration for both labour and education has been essential to many families, although on different scales. Contemporary practices of student migration are partly related to the aspirations of an expanding middle-class, whose status is derived, at least in part, from its exposure to transnational cultural forces (Liechty 2003). In the subsequent paragraphs, I argue that middle-class families today orient themselves towards broader geographical horizons, which has opened up new destinations such as Denmark.

Geographical mobility which is an integrated practice of many Nepalese households is reflected in several ways. First, labour migration to India, dating back to the eighteenth century, has long been integral to the sustenance of agricultural households in Nepal either through seasonal rural labour or through long-lasting wage labour arrangements, including recruitment into the British and later the Indian armies (Sharma 2008). As mentioned earlier, and as later examples will further demonstrate, migratory circuits have expanded radically over the last two decades and now transcend national borders throughout the world (see, e.g. Bruslé 2009/10). Family homes are often spread across many locations, both within and outside Nepal, but family members usually remain part of the larger social group and responsible for supporting each other, however dispersed the physical relations may be. Although it is beyond the scope of this article to go further into this aspect, the example of student migration demonstrates that such support is far from limited to immediate financial contributions, but also includes more delayed rewards in terms of increased status and credentials gained from an education abroad, which will also benefit the family. Such patterns of translocal livelihoods and diversification of economic and social resources are also reflected among the Nepalese students in Denmark; many of whom come from families with homes and land in different parts of Nepal, typically one in an urban area of Central and Southern Nepal, and one in the hilly, rural areas. Similarly, several reported to have grown up with a father working in India as a civil servant or in the army, and to have relatives of their own generation living in Australia, US, UK and Ireland, to mention just a few places.

Second, access to formal education in Nepal has been and still is conditioned by the ability to be geographically mobile. Historically produced caste- and class-based inequalities in Nepal have been reinforced by the mountainous character of the country, which has limited access to education in remote areas and compelled young people who are striving for a continued formal education to be geographically mobile. Children often had to walk several hours to get to school, and as they moved up the educational ladder, they had to travel further necessitating moving away from their local community. Several Nepalese students in Denmark also did their primary and sometimes secondary schooling in the village, moving first to provincial towns for high school, then to the larger cities for their college education and eventually abroad for higher education.

While the ability to be geographically mobile has been and still is an important factor in obtaining access to formal education at various levels, it is evident that migration with the purpose of studying abroad in the context of contemporary Nepal is a middle-class privilege. Although middle-class status is notoriously difficult to identify in objective terms (Liechty 2003, 64), there are in a Nepalese context some common features. First, it is dependent on a relatively solid position in the socio-economic hierarchy, which can be identified through certain interrelated markers: land holdings across Nepal, the position of male relatives (e.g. as politicians, lawyers, businessmen, government officials and teachers), and the economic resources to pay for an education abroad, or at least to raise the money needed for the travel, initial stay and deposit required to cover the first year's fees. It is a segment of Nepalese society which is affluent enough to make the initial investment in its children's education abroad and to survive without remittances, yet which is unable fully to support them on a regular basis. Second, middle-class status is based on a self-ascribed identity and it is therefore a very heterogeneous social category (Dickey 2012, 562) defined by the varying ways in which people consider themselves to belong to the 'middle'. Some explicitly distinguished themselves from those migrating to India, the Middle East and Malaysia, countries which are known for recruiting a significant number of unskilled manual labourers. In the words of Hem,[3] a returnee whom I met in Kathmandu: 'It is not possible [to study abroad] if your family is not from the middle-class or upper middle-class. People won't be able to send them [their children] to foreign countries.'[4] His family was sufficiently privileged for his father to have been able to give him 10 lakh Nepali Rupees (approximately 8500 Euros) before he went to Denmark in 2008, enough to cover travel and the initial fees.

The choice of destination is linked to prevailing perceptions of available opportunities with regard to education, jobs and prospects for onward travel, all within a widely shared hierarchy of migrant destinations where India sits at the bottom, the Middle East and Far East occupy the middle ground and finally Europe, Australia and North America on the top. Many had only vague ideas of Denmark before coming and in several cases it was apparent that Denmark figures both as a destination in itself and as an entrance point to Europe. Take Uddhab, who in response to my question of why he had chosen Denmark for his studies promptly answered that he had not come to Denmark *per se*, but to Europe, which Nepalese students thought would be easily accessible thanks to the open borders within the Schengen area. Others considered Denmark a peaceful, democratic society, and yet others had no prior knowledge of the country and, like in the case of Prakash described in the next paragraph, came to know about it through college advertisements in Nepalese newspapers.

When I met Prakash in early summer 2012 he had spent 5 years in Denmark and was now in a 'top up' Bachelor programme. He was born and grew up in a small town in the hills of Western Nepal with his mother and siblings, while his father worked in India as a technician for the Indian Army. His father retired in the mid-1990s after 20 years of service and opened a veterinary clinic to supplement his pension from the Indian Army. Having studied commerce at Bachelor's level in the early 2000s in Butwal, a large city in Southern Nepal, Prakash got what he considered a good job as a computer assistant at the Military Pension Branch of the Indian Embassy in Pokhara, responsible for distributing pensions to Nepalese ex-army personnel from the Indian army. He stayed there for 2 years with his wife, but the sight of his friends progressing in their careers and going abroad, motivated him to look for opportunities outside Nepal. His priorities were Australia, UK and *of course US*, as he expressed it, but an advertisement for a computer science programme at a business college in Denmark caught his attention and he eventually decided to apply for it. The choice of Denmark, thus, was somewhat incidental in the sense that he did not opt for this country in particular, but it was where an opportunity presented itself. He explained why he had decided to go abroad:

> ...I was doing quite a good job in Nepal. That was of course a good job for average Nepalese people, you know, to work in an embassy. And I got an apartment for my wife and me to live [at the Embassy], so it was not so bad [KV noted that yet he decided to give up the job to go abroad]. Yeah, of course I thought of other friends. Some of those I studied with are doctors and some of them are engineers. So I thought, oh I will be stuck here if I continue my job, you know. Every day was the same work. There was no...like good knowledge to gain but of course I had to use my brain but still...like every day it was the same job I was doing. I was fed up so then I decided, ok I will, if I get some opportunity I will go abroad and study.

It was the quest for intellectual stimulation and fear of getting stuck, combined with his constantly comparing himself to his peer, who had moved ahead both career-wise and in terms of attractive countries in the hierarchy of migrant destinations, which in Prakash's own explanation made him migrate to Denmark for an education.

Similar concerns about being left behind in Nepal were expressed by Suman, who came to Denmark in 2004 at the age of 22. At the time he was about to complete his Bachelor's degree from Nepal, he was keen to leave the country. He also learned about the educational opportunities in Denmark from an advertisement in the newspaper. In his own words, he did 'not know anything at all' about Denmark. Although his family had not been directly involved in the armed conflict, the general situation of uncertainty reinforced his desire to leave the country:

> I always wanted to explore something new. I wanted to get out of Nepal...just to try something new. And because of the political situation I wanted to go and try something new. And youngsters want to try and go abroad. That could be the reason why so many people are moving out. That's how I came here.

He belonged to a well-travelled family. His younger brother was also studying in Denmark and his cousins were in the UK and US studying medicine, which in his view put pressure on other young people in the family. Like Prakash, he was convinced that he would be able to get a well-paid job if he returned to Nepal. Thus he had obtained technical qualifications in the field of solar energy, a potential solution to recurrent problems of electricity supply in present-day Nepal. Securing a decent standard of living in Kathmandu would not be a problem, he assured me, partly because his wife's family owned a house where they could stay. At the same time he recognised that having seen 'the rest of the world', as he expressed it, made him compare life in Denmark and Nepal, and the aftermath of the armed conflict – recurrent strikes and political instability – was a major contributing factor in his and his wife's decision not to return to Nepal after he completed his undergraduate degree, as he had initially planned.

A central theme in these examples is the orientation towards broader horizons, which is both an important motivation for and outcome of migration. The young men all spoke about experiences of having seen and learned from the world around them, both through and beyond institutions of formal education. Showing how migration for education provides a frame for Nepalese middle-class youth to explore the world, their reflections point to an often overlooked aspect of migration from poorer regions of the world to the global North. However, acknowledging the intrinsic relationship between learning and livelihood pathways, and the role that geographical mobility plays in this (Froerer and Portisch 2012), it is obvious that migration for education is also expected to pay off in terms of academic qualifications, a diploma and better job opportunities and, thus, in a longer perspective to help improve the family's social status. The 'student' identity conferred by this particular kind of migration is, as the next section will reveal, fundamental for Nepalese migrants' claims to preserve their middle-class status in Denmark because it allows for a reinterpretation of other available social identities.

Maintaining a position in 'the middle'

Class positions are fundamentally unstable, not just because they are vulnerable to economic fluctuations, but also because they must be recognised by others (Dickey 2012, 595–596). A position in 'the middle' thus requires continuous efforts to maintain one's status in situations where it can be challenged. As Mark Liechty (2003) points out, based on his work on urban middle-class youths in Nepal in the early 1990s, ideas of respectability and honour (*ijjat*) were central to the emergence of the middle-class. What this means in specific terms obviously changes over time and tends to differ for men and women. However, the idea of *ijjat* as something almost tangible that can be gained or lost and which is inextricably linked to both material and moral domains (Liechty 2003, 83–85) is equally relevant for the present study. In this section, I ask what this quest for maintaining a position in 'the middle' means in the context of transnational mobility. More precisely, how Nepalese students and their spouses deal with their simultaneous positions as, on one the hand, international students and, on the other hand, low-skilled workers dependent upon a steady income to earn a living in Denmark.

Representing the Nepalese as a problematic category of poor, foreign students and accusing them for working illegally, the Danish media have recurrently questioned the intentions behind their reasons for coming to Denmark and blamed them for being essentially labour migrants, who use their student visas only as tickets into the Danish labour market (Valentin 2012b). Such accusations reflect dilemmas arising from blurred boundaries between a commercialised, globally expanding education market and an unregulated labour market that depends on low-skilled, low-paid foreigners. Students from outside Europe are allowed to work 60 hours per month and full time in the months of June, July and August, when colleges are closed. Students are occasionally deported from Denmark because they have worked more than their allotted 60 hours. Such deportations tend to reinforce suspicion surrounding this form of migration. Furthermore, they generate much anxiety as well as occasional accusations among the students of having reported each other to the authorities. Spouses may work full time throughout the year, thus there is an obvious economic advantage for those who manage to get their partner to Denmark. The work available is mostly in the service sector – kitchen work, cleaning and house-keeping – often for low wages and at odd hours. This kind of work is new to many students and is implicitly captured in a comment by Anita, a student and part-time house-keeper, who told me that it was only after she came to Denmark that she started to ask herself what kind of people do such jobs in Nepal; she then pondered aloud: '…the poor, the uneducated?' Some students had work experi-ence from Nepal, but as teachers, journalists and in various white-collar positions or in a family business.

The perception of Nepalese students as 'immigrants', strongly nurtured by the media, is given credence by the fact that most of them live in areas inhabited by many immigrants, mostly Muslims. I have often heard students, especially those with small children, stress that they would like to move to supposedly safer areas of Copenhagen with fewer foreigners. Explicitly concluding that it is an outcome of too strong a Muslim presence in the area, several people have, for example, mentioned to me the case of a Nepalese child who returned from the kindergarten telling his parents that he would no longer eat pork. General reservations regarding 'Muslims' can partly be explained by the ambivalent experiences that many have had, especially with Pakistanis. On the one hand, there is a sense of a shared identity as South Asians, but on the other hand the Pakistanis have, by virtue of being a relatively consolidated category of immigrants in Denmark, attained a situation both on the housing and the labour market that has left the Nepalese in a structurally inferior position. Particularly during the early stages of their stay in Denmark, many Nepalese are dependent upon Pakistani house owners and employers, often on quite dubious contracts with little security of tenure and unregulated tariffs, which have frequently left the students in vulnerable situations. Later, as they build wider networks and learn to navigate Danish institutions, including housing companies, many move on to more organised, permanent forms of accommodation, yet still mostly in the same areas, where the available housing is.

In many respects, the lives of Nepalese students resemble that of most Danish students: they go to college, work part-time, establish families and enjoy the social life of students. However, being dependent upon manual wage-labour, they are positioned in a social category, which does not mirror their social position in Nepal. It is against this social and economic backdrop that Nepalese students' claims to be middle-class and the demand for a student identity must be understood. These claims and demands are, as the following two examples will show and similar to observations made by Radha Adhikari (2009/10) among Nepalese nurses in UK, reinforced by students' and others' expectations that their stay abroad should lead to some concrete achievements, in this case in the form of academic degrees.

Mahesh, who in his own words is 'totally from the village', came to Denmark to study in 2006 and had to pay a year's tuition fee of 50,000 DKK (app. 6700 Euro) in advance. He explained that he had got 'credit' from his parents, but not in the sense of a loan to be repaid in money. Anticipating that he would not be able to get a job if they provided him with a Nepalese education, his parents, Mahesh claimed, saw an education abroad, although much more expensive, as a 'once and for all' investment from which they would also benefit further down the line, when Mahesh would take care of them. When I interviewed him in April 2012, he was about to complete his Bachelor's degree and had plans to visit Nepal with his wife and daughter. However, he was not yet ready to go because:

> ...before I go I want to make sure that I get admission into a master [programme]. In Nepal education is like social status...if I go now I can say I have finished bachelor...after six months I can say I'm doing master.

Likewise Sabita, the wife of Uddhab referred to earlier, touched upon the importance of completing her education in Denmark. She came to Denmark as a newly wedded spouse in 2008 and for the first couple of years she worked, first in a restaurant and later as a hotel maid, to support her husband's studies. In 2010, however, the roles reversed: Sabita began to study and became the primary visa bearer whereas Uddhab became the 'dependent' and full-time breadwinner. Like several other couples they switched between these positions for, as Sabita said, the main reason for their parents' approval of their decision to leave Nepal was the education they would get – her parents would 'kill her' if she dropped out of her studies. In response to my question whether her parents supported her studies financially she answered that as a middle-class family they could not afford it, and added that she and her husband were not able to meet their parents' expectations of immediate financial returns as their earnings just barely covered all expenses in Denmark.

It is difficult to strike a balance between meeting the expectations of the family in Nepal, both short and long-term, and maintaining a living as a student in Denmark, which includes not only housing, food and fees, but also going out, buying new mobile phones and travel. It is essential for most Nepalese to work, but the work available to them in Denmark is generally of a sort that they would never consider doing in Nepal, because it does not correspond to their idea of a proper occupation for people of their 'level' in society. Kumar, a returnee student whom I met in Kathmandu, told me that he would never have worked as a cleaner in Nepal and he did not tell anyone that he had done that kind of work in a Danish kindergarten. Yet, he seemed to have come to terms with it by interpreting his work from the perspective of Danish society:

> ...it was frustrating the first time you know. There were no choices, you know, so I thought it doesn't matter here in Denmark because there is no discrimination in work here in Denmark. All the Danish are doing this so why can't I do. So I was thinking in terms of Danish [people] not Nepalese, you know.

The ambiguous experience of having to maintain a balance between preserving one's educated middle-class status in Nepal and working as a cleaner in Denmark was expressed by Sunita, a woman in her twenties, who came to Denmark as a spouse in 2009. Like several other female spouses, she left Nepal part-way through her studies and her initial plan, she told me, was to stay only for a short time in Denmark and then return to complete her Bachelor's degree, but soon after her arrival she became pregnant and therefore stayed on. She expressed a keen interest in going back to Nepal to complete her education. She was concerned about how she as a middle-class woman coped with her current social position in Denmark. She had previously worked in a fast-food restaurant, but due to her limited Danish skills only in the kitchen. She was currently working for a cleaning company three hours every weekday. Except for that, she explained, she spent most of her time at home, taking care of her one-year-old son and studying to finish her Bachelor's degree in Nepal. She had found it very difficult to come to Denmark in the first place because:

> ...the life style in Nepal and here is so different. In our Nepal women don't 'struggle' in this way [...]. They don't do this kind of work. Most of us who come here are 'medium' family. There are no 'high class', and the 'low class' cannot come. Our Nepali women don't do this kind of work [...] They work at home and do a bit of office work (*jagir*) but after we come here we're all doing cleaning [...]. It is about honour (*ijjat*), but another thing is that people who have studied up to our level, if I have done a master, I can go for a position [in Nepal] through the Public Service Commission. With a master I could apply for any government job, but in Nepal you don't earn much from these jobs. People of our level (*hamro level ko manche*) don't do much of this.

Sunita's account represents a gendered perspective on what she considers an imbalance in her Nepalese status as an educated, middle-class woman and her Danish status as a cleaner. Informed by Nepalese ideas of honour and femininity, Nepalese women's mobility is generally more restricted than that of men and is tied up with a set of expectations regarding suitable behaviour and future trajectories for women, which conflict with the jobs that are available to them. At the same time, these notions capture a more general underlying issue of respectability that may be articulated differently by men and women, but which are intrinsic to their middle-class position and mediated, to a great extent, through an educated status. In other words, it is through their claims to an educated status that they can perform their middle-class-ness and thus maintain a sense of dignity in a context where they may otherwise be taken for 'ordinary' immigrants – i.e. potential labour migrants.

Conclusion

This article has examined how ideas of education figure in processes of social and geographical mobility in the case of contemporary student migration from Nepal to Denmark, and how claims to an educated status help people maintain a sense of respectability in a context which offers different and sometimes conflicting social identities. Historically speaking, access to formal education in Nepal has to a large extent been conditioned by the ability to be geographically mobile, but the scale of such geographical mobility differs greatly depending on social class. Migration for education abroad, especially to Europe, North America and Australia, is a middle-class privilege, that has allowed certain segments of the Nepalese youth to escape a post-conflict situation, where educational and occupational opportunities for young people have diminished considerably. As I have shown in this article, current practices of student migration from Nepal to Denmark have been fuelled by an expanding international, and highly commercialised, education market which combined with people's enduring faith in the prospects of formal education has opened up new locations and possible pathways for the middle-class.

Shedding light on the relationship among geographical mobility, class-based identities and education, the article has shown, first, that it is crucial to take into account historically anchored, socio-cultural mobility practices, which contribute to the shaping of individual and collective trajectories. Individual educational trajectories are reflections of and embedded within wider mobility practices that have long been central to the livelihoods of many Nepalese families. Current forms of student migration, instigated by the marketisation of international education, must therefore be seen as geographical extensions of the already existing practices through which certain segments of the population can claim membership in a transnational, educated middle-class.

Second, acknowledging that the middle-class is a subjectively experienced category (Dickey 2012), which gains its meaning from the particular socio-historical contexts in which it is embedded, the article has illustrated that geographical mobility may challenge well-known class-based positions and compel people to reclaim and accentuate their middle-class status as a means of coping with a situation where their social status is at stake. To approach this through the lens of student migration emphasises the way in which social identities are negotiated and reinterpreted in mobility processes because the student category itself, imbued with respectability, hope and future prospects, challenges dominant ideas of migration from the global South as a primarily lower-class phenomenon. Insisting on a student identity is therefore also a way to distinguish oneself from other categories of migrants and to counter the often negative stereotypes associated with them. Focusing on the production of middle-class identity associated with educational achievements gained from a study abroad, this article has contributed to challenge dominant approaches to student migration from the global South to the global North, yet without ignoring the structural inequalities that lie beneath contemporary processes of globalisation and the forces that produce mobility and immobility.

Notes

1. The project is part of a collaborative project, 'Education, Mobility and Citizenship. An Anthropological Study of Educational Migration to Denmark' supported by the Danish Council for Independent Research, Humanities, under grant 10 080278.
2. As per fourth quarter of 2013. Information retrieved from Danmarks Statistik http://www.statistikbanken.dk/FOLK1, 3 June 2013.
3. In order to secure anonymity all names of informants are pseudonyms.
4. Interviews have been conducted in a mix of English, Nepali and Danish. For the readability interview quotations have been slightly edited grammatically.

References

Adhikari, R. 2009/10. "The 'Dream Trap': Brokering, 'Study Abroad' and Nurse Migration from Nepal to UK." *European Bulletin of Himalayan Research* 35 36: 122 138.

Baas, M. 2007. "The Language of Migration: The Education Industry Versus the Migration Industry." *People and Place* 15 (2): 49 60.

Bhattarai, K. 2011. "Brain Gain (Drain), Immigration and Global Network: Nepalese Students in the UK." *International Journal of Economic Policy in Emerging Economies* 4 (4): 345 365. doi:10.1504/IJEPEE.2011.043309.

Biao, X., and W. Shen. 2009. "International Student Migration and Social Stratification in China." *International Journal of Educational Development* 29: 513 522. doi:10.1016/ j.ijedudev.2009.04.006.

Brooks, R., and J. Waters. 2011. *Student Mobilities, Migration and the Internationalization of Higher Education.* London: Palgrave Macmillan.

Bruslé, T., ed. 2009/10. "Nepali Migrations." *European Bulletin of Himalayan Research* 35 36.

Dickey, S. 2012. "The Pleasures and Anxieties of Being in the Middle: Emerging Middle Class Identities in Urban South India." *Modern Asian Studies* 46 (3): 559 599. doi:10.1017/S0026749X11000333.

Fernandes, L. 2011. "Hegemony and Inequality: Theoretical Reflections on India's 'New' Middle Class." In *Elite and Everyman. The Cultural Politics of the Indian Middle Class,* edited by A. Baviskar and R. Ray, 58 82. London: Routledge.

Froerer, P., and A. Portisch. 2012. "Introduction to the Special Issue: Learning, Livelihoods, and Social Mobility." *Anthropology and Education Quarterly* 43 (4): 332 343. doi:10.1111/j.1548 1492.2012.01188.x.

Gurung, G., and J. Adhikhari. 2004. "Nepal: The Prospects and Problems of Foreign Labour Migration." In *Migrant Workers and Human Rights: Out Migration from South Asia,* edited by P. S. Ahn, 100 130. New Delhi: International Labour Organization.

Kollmair, M., S. Manandhar, B. Subedi, and S. Thieme. 2006. "New Figures for Old Stories: Migration and Remittances in Nepal." *Migration Letters* 3 (2): 151 160.

Lem, W., and P. G. Barber. 2010. "Introduction." In *Class, Contention, and a World in Motion,* edited by W. Lem and P. G. Barber, 1 20. New York: Berghanh.

Liechty, M. 2003. *Suitably Modern: Making Middle Class Culture in a New Consumer Society.* Princeton, NJ: Princeton University Press.

Neilson, B. 2009. "The World Seen from a Taxi: Students Migrants Workers in the Global Multiplication of Labour." *Subjectivity* 29: 425 444. doi:10.1057/sub.2009.23.

Pan, D. 2011. "Student Visas, Undocumented Labour, and the Boundaries of Legality: Chinese Migration and English as a Foreign Language Education in the Republic of Ireland." *Social Anthropology* 19 (3): 268 287. doi:10.1111/j.1469 8676.2011.00159.x.

Seddon, D., J. Adhikari, and G. Gurung. 2002. "Foreign Labor Migration and the Remittance Economy of Nepal." *Critical Asian Studies* 34 (1): 19 40. doi:10.1080/ 146727102760166581.

Sharma, J. R. 2008. "Practices of Male Labor Migration from the Hills of Nepal to India in Development Discourses: Which Pathology?" *Gender, Technology and Development* 12 (3): 303 323. doi:10.1177/097185240901200302.

Sijapati, B. 2009/10. "Nepali Transmigrants: An Examination of Transnational Ties among Nepali Immigrants in the United States." *European Bulletin of Himalayan Research* 35 36: 139 153.

Thieme, S. and U. Müller Böker. 2004. "Financial Self Help Associations among Far West Nepalese Labor Migrants in Delhi, India." *Asian and Pacific Migration Journal* 13 (3): 339 361.

Udlændingeservice [The Immigration Service]. 2009. *Tal og fakta på udlændingeområdet 2008* [Numbers and Facts on Immigration 2008]. Denmark: Ministeriet for Flygtninge, Indvandrere og Integration [The Ministry for Refugees, Immigrants and Integration].

Udlændingestyrelsen [The Immigration Board]. 2013. *Tal og fakta på udlændingeområdet 2012* [Numbers and Facts on Immigration 2012]. Copenhagen: The Immigration Board.

Valentin, K. 2005. *Schooled for the Future? Educational Policy and Everyday Life among Urban Squatters in Nepal.* Greenwich, CT: Information Age.

Valentin, K. 2012a. "The Role of Education in Mobile Livelihoods: Social and Geographical Routes of Young Nepalese Migrants in India." *Anthropology and Education Quarterly* 43 (4): 429 442. doi:10.1111/j.1548 1492.2012.01195.x.

Valentin, K. 2012b. "Caught between Internationalisation and Immigration: The Case of Nepalese Students in Denmark." *Learning and Teaching: The International Journal of Higher Education in the Social Sciences* 5 (3): 56 74. doi:10.3167/latiss.2012.050304.

Becoming independent through au pair migration: self-making and social re-positioning among young Filipinas in Denmark

Karina Märcher Dalgas

Over the past decade, growing numbers of young Filipinas have entered Denmark on the au pair scheme. While its official aim is to broaden the cultural horizons of youth, researchers generally view Filipina au pairing as a form of labour migration using au pairs as inexpensive domestic workers. This article argues that, despite this critique, au pairing does play an impor tant formative role for young Filipinas because it opens up for experiences abroad that enable them to be recognised as independent adults in Philippine society. Rather than autonomy, however, au pairs define their independence in terms of their capacity to assume responsibility for others, thereby achiev ing a position of social respect. Based on ethnographic fieldwork in Denmark and the Philippines, this article explores how young Filipinas use the social, economic, and cultural resources they gain from their au pair stay abroad to re position themselves vis à vis family and friends at home.

Introduction

Since 2000, more than 13,500 young Filipinos[1] have been au pairs in Denmark. The Danish authorities categorise au pairs as a kind of foreign students who 'broaden their cultural horizons' by staying with a Danish host family. This educational purpose entails the assumption that exposure to another culture and society will allow young people to develop themselves personally, and au pair placement is thus thought to offer a formative experience for them. The au pair scheme, however, is also used as a domestic work arrangement because au pairs must perform domestic chores in exchange for room and board at the host family as well as pocket money. While the amount of money is small it allows the migrants to send remittances back home. A prevailing theme in the literature on au pairs is the vulnerability caused by the au pairs' ambiguous position as, officially, students of culture and language in their host society, members of their host families and, as de facto workers (see for example, Hess and Puckhaber 2004; Mellini et al., 2007; Anderson 2007). While this clearly is an important topic of investigation, little attention has been paid to the educational aspects of the au pair program. This article sheds light on this dimension of au pair migration by exploring how young Filipina au pairs in Denmark see their stay abroad as an avenue of personal development and recognition. Such development, I will show, cannot be gauged in terms of Danish (or Western European) ideas of what constitutes a proper cultural exchange program. Rather, it must be understood within the framework of Philippine notions of the significance of formative journeys for young people.

By focusing on the educational aspects of au pairing, I follow the call by Johnson and Werbner to 'move beyond a conceptual framework that treats women international migrants simply as a victimized labor diaspora' (Johnson and Werbner 2010, 208). I do this by building on studies that examines the role of Filipino migration as a pathway to self-transformation. In a study of migration from the Philippines, Aguilar observes that it is a common notion that the struggles migrants face abroad allow them 'to perceive themselves as "objectively" altered beings' (1999, 106). McKay (2012) and Bulloch (2009) point to how such personal transformation can take on local forms. In her study from Siquijor, Bulloch emphasises how migration is regarded as a pathway towards becoming modern and cosmopolitan (2009), whereas McKay highlights the fact that villagers from Haliap view migration as a way to become recognised as 'big persons' in their local communities and attain a position of respect in the family (2012). Migrants' self-making is thus significant for the character of their social relations with family members back home.

The large body of literature on the transnational family ties of Filipina migrants has paid special attention to the painful separation of migrated mothers and their left-behind children (see, for example, Alipio 2009; Pratt 2009). Less interest has been shown in the migration of young, single Filipinas without children, how they experience leaving home, how their relations with family back home evolve and what kind of possibilities they associate with going abroad. These are central topics in this analysis of au pair migration to Denmark. By focusing on women who are 18–30 years old, unmarried and without children (which are all requirements for enrolment in the programme), I explore how young people, who have not yet achieved a status as adults in their home societies can use their stay abroad as au pairs to gain recognition as mature women. They do so by demonstrating that they have become, on the one hand, financially able persons who can contribute to the family and who are dependable and, on the other, independent adults who are able to manage on their own without parental protection. Through their migration the au pairs thus re-position themselves in relation to their neighbours and family members. This social re-positioning takes place both within family hierarchies, for example when au pairs receive greater decision-making power in relation to relatives left behind and in wider Philippine society where migration is viewed as a pathway to becoming a respected person with prestigious experiences and valuable knowledge of life in Western countries.

This article is based on ethnographic fieldwork conducted in 2011–2012 among current and former au pairs in the greater Copenhagen area (Denmark) and among former and prospective au pairs in the Philippines, mainly on the Visayan island of Bohol. In the Philippines, I visited families of au pairs and former au pairs, and while the interviews with former, current and prospective au pairs were conducted in English, I received help from former au pairs acting as translators during many of the interviews with the au pairs' family members. In order to examine the personal development that the young migrants associate with being au pairs, this article highlights how prospective au pairs explain their expectations of going abroad and how, in their narratives, former au pairs present their experience of migration as a path to self-transformation. Thus, while many of them said that they would migrate or had migrated to help family back home, they also described their stay abroad as a way to see the world and become independent. In the Philippines, this formative dimension of travel abroad became apparent, not only in stories told with reference to au pair placement, but also in accounts of other migration experiences, both national and international. This suggests that youth migration more broadly plays a key role in the attainment of adult status in Philippine society.

The ambiguous au pair program: policy change and perspectives from a Philippine village

Although au pair regulations vary in different countries, the au pair scheme in general is based on the European au pair convention of 1969. This agreement encourages member countries to ensure that au pairs receive 'special protection relating to the material or moral conditions found in the receiving country', considering that 'many of the persons [au pairs] are minors deprived for a long period of support of their families' (Council of Europe 1969). This points to an expectation that au pairs will be included in their host family. At the same time, the convention defines au pairs as belonging 'neither to the student category nor to the worker category but to a special category which has features of both' (Council of Europe 1969). The Danish regulations are based on this definition and thus offer au pairs an ambiguous position as family members, workers, students and – due to the cultural exchange purpose of the program – tourists. The au pair-worker element consists in the requirement that au pairs conduct domestic chores in the host families they live with for a maximum of 30 hours a week and that they receive in return food, lodging and a monthly allowance of DKK 3250 (€435) monthly. The categorisation of au pairs as a kind of foreign student in Denmark means that they receive neither work permits nor workers' rights. Nevertheless, the au pair scheme has been criticised for, essentially, being a domestic work arrangement that circumvents the Danish ban on immigration by domestic workers by categorising au pairs as a form of foreign students temporarily resident in Denmark (Stenum 2011). The au pairs that I have interviewed also regard au pairing as a kind of domestic work migration that allows them to send remittances back home – a perspective that is strengthened by the importance of domestic work as an occupational sphere for Filipina migrants abroad.

Several scholars have noticed that the ambiguous position leaves au pairs vulnerable to labour exploitation (Hess and Puckhaber 2004; Yodanis and Lauer 2005). For this reason, The Philippine Overseas Employment Administration (POEA) banned au pair migration to Europe in 1998 after several reports of under-compensation, excessive working hours, abuse and even prostitution (Stenum 2011, 34). While the ban was imposed to protect au pairs from being used as domestic workers, the Philippine authorities also encouraged European countries to instead 'negotiate bilateral agreements on migrant domestic workers programmes' (Stenum 2011, 33). The Danish authorities ignored the ban and in 2008, when the number of au pair permits peaked, 2163 Philippine citizens received Danish au pair permits (Grunnet and Binder 2014, 42). In October 2010, after months of diplomatic negotiations, the ban was lifted for Norway, Denmark and Switzerland. Paradoxically, while the Danish authorities still refused to recognise au pairs as workers, the Philippine authorities required that prospective au pairs should go through procedures at POEA, which administers the employment of Philippine nationals abroad. In 2012, the Philippines lifted the ban for the whole of Europe, and the Commission on Filipinos Overseas (CFO) declared that au pairs no longer needed to go through the POEA, as they were considered to be participants in a cultural and educational exchange (Commission on Filipinos Overseas 2012a).

These legal changes seemingly have had no impact on the scale of Filipina au pair migration to Denmark, which is mostly facilitated through the au pairs' personal networks. On Bohol, I thus visited two neighbourhoods in the towns of Loboc and Dagohoy where au pair placement to Denmark had become a well-established migration route for young women. Since an au pair can stay in Denmark for a maximum of 2 years, younger siblings often replace older siblings when the contract expires. By not asking for recruitment fees,[2] and by lending the money necessary to embark upon this migration, these siblings – or other family recruiters – have enabled women from relatively poor families to become au pairs. It is common for Filipina au pairs in Denmark to remit approximately DKK 1000–1500 (€134–200) per month. Only three of the 34 current and former au pairs interviewed came from families that did not rely on remittances. The families of au pairs that I visited in the Philippines generally had crops and livestock for subsistence purposes, but needed remittances to pay for medicine, house repairs and tertiary education. For the young people who enrolled in the au pair scheme it therefore became a way to act as family breadwinners. In these villages au pair placement is generally considered a good way for young women to migrate. One mother of an au pair, for example, explained that she initially disapproved of her daughter's plans to go to Denmark, because she herself had bad memories of the hard labour she had performed as a domestic worker in Manila during her youth. She changed her mind, however, when she learned that an au pair is expected to have a light work load. Several former and prospective au pairs also emphasised this as a positive aspect of the scheme, and au pair placement was commonly referred to as 'domestic work light'. Moreover, some parents explained that they felt it was safer to send their young daughters to Denmark than to Singapore or Hong Kong, where stories of harsh abuse were frequent.

During my fieldwork I met many au pairs who worked more than the stipulated maximum of 30 hours weekly, and some pointed out that their labour was far more demanding than the 'light household chores' stated in their contracts. For most au pairs, cleaning the host family home was the heaviest and most time-consuming task. They often used the term 'Cinderella day' to describe the busy Mondays, where they do 'general cleaning' after they – and the host family – have had the weekend off. These cleaning tasks are often physically strenuous, and it is questionable whether they fall into the category of 'light household chores'.

Despite this use of the Cinderella analogy to describe the hard labour and the low status connected to cleaning, au pairing in Denmark was generally viewed in very positive terms in the Philippines. Former au pairs, who also had work experience from Singapore, thus described their au pair placement in Denmark as significantly safer and less labour intensive. Their very positive descriptions of their au pair experiences could, however, also stem from their reluctance to talk about their troubles abroad, because they did not want to worry their parents. Moreover, by presenting their migration narratives as stories of success, they sustained the image as people who had 'made it' abroad. Still, it is worth noticing that the regulatory perception of au pairs as non-workers does, in practice, influence the au pairs' actual workload. If au pairs were given only two hours of leisure time daily, which is common among domestic workers in Southern Europe, it would be an example of gross abuse of the au pair scheme. Thus, while Danish labour unions, Western scholars, and the Philippine authorities point to the risk of exploitation as a result of the ambiguity of the scheme, the villagers on Bohol generally view au pairing as a form of domestic work migration that offers good conditions for young women.

Youth travel as formative: au pair placement in a historical perspective

Despite the economic incentives that motivate young Filipinas to become au pairs, their participation in the scheme may still conform to the official purpose of the au pair program, which is to enable young people to broaden their cultural horizons and therefore develop themselves personally. However, it is necessary to take into consideration how understandings of proper personal development may vary cross-culturally and over time. Thus, at different times in the past, au pairing has been associated with personal development towards different ends. The first au pair positions can be traced back to nineteenth-century Switzerland, when bourgeois families began to recruit women of similar social standing to care for their children (Boer 1987, 20). These women could not be treated as servants and, therefore, did not receive salaries, but were instead 'au pair,' meaning they attained a position 'on equal terms' with the family members. By learning a foreign language and housekeeping in a different culture, the au pairs were able to use their stay to become attractive marriage partners. Not until the turn of the nineteenth century, as it became appropriate for bourgeois women to obtain work as nannies and governesses, did au pair placement prepare young people for salaried employment (Boer 1987, 21).

Until the mid-1990s, Denmark was primarily an 'au pair-sending' country. Au pairing by Danes is popularly framed as a *dannelsesrejse* (Larsen 2004) which translates as a formative or *Bildungs* journey, and thus brings the educational aspects of the experience to the fore. *Dannelsesrejsen* has connotations of the Grand Tour, the educational journey to specific places of cultural interest in Europe that was an integral part of British gentlemanly education from the seventeenth to the nineteenth century (Brauer 1959, 190). Through the Grand Tour, young members of the upper classes were exposed to European high culture, becoming cosmopolitan and learning the manners of 'cultured' men, thus preparing themselves for adult life in the European elites (Brauer 1959). Viewed as a formative journey, an au pair stay is also intended to prepare young people for adult life, but whereas this implied a good marriage for the early bourgeois au pairs, it later came to mean obtaining qualifications for paid domestic work, as this became an acceptable career path for middle-class women. This shows how mobility, depending on local values and power hierarchies, is suffused with different forms of meaning cross-culturally. The point is that these journeys are formative of different ends, as they help young people acquire skills associated with being an adult in their respective societies of origin. Thus, to understand the formative dimensions of au pair migration, we need to explore the particular abilities and qualifications that are associated with being respected adult women in the au pairs' home societies.

There are no statistics showing the number of au pairs coming to Denmark before the scheme was opened to non-EU members in the mid-1990s.[3] There are, however, stories of young Scandinavians who were au pairs in Denmark 50 years ago, and according to officials at the government au pair office, a number of Baltic women were au pairs in Denmark during the 1990s. By the end of the millennium, an increasing number of Filipinas were embarking on Danish au pair placement, and today more than 80% of the au pairs in Denmark are of Philippine origin. Considering the importance of migration among middle-class Philippine families, I suggest that the tight-knit family economies and the prestige associated with people who have travelled abroad are central aspects of this preparation for adulthood.

Au pair migration as a way to personal success

Long-distance migration from the Philippines took off in the early nineteenth century and by the 1930s more than 100,000 Filipinos were working in the United States (Rodriguez 2010, 4). In the early 1970s President Ferdinand Marcos introduced systematic labour export policies, and today labour emigration has been institutionalised in the Philippines for more than 50 years. Thus, in the words of Rodrigues, Filipinos are 'the most globalized workforce on the planet' (Rodriguez 2010, 141), counting approximately 10.45 million Filipino citizens, or about 10% of the population, who live in 227 different countries (Commission on Filipinos Overseas 2012b). Despite the global financial crisis, the total value of remittances sent by Filipinos abroad continues to increase, amounting to about US$23 billion in 2013 (Bangko Sentral ng Pilipinas 2014). These remittances not only are a cornerstone of the national economy but also create a necessary income for a large part of the Philippine middle classes.

National labour export policies have fuelled a 'culture of migration' (Asis 2006), where migration has been normalised as an important livelihood option in the Philippines (Barber 2004, 204). Indeed, aspirations to migrate overseas are widespread in Philippine society. These aspirations, I suggest, are also framed by understandings of migration as a way that prospective migrants aim to live up to local notions of personal success that point towards the transformative potential of migration. The importance of migration as a livelihood option affects how young, middle-class Filipinos think about their future, and what they imagine they can become by going abroad. In order to understand ideas of personal success through migration I find Edberg's (2004) concept of 'cultural persona' useful. He defines it as a 'culturally shaped, flexible public representation ... that is embodied in a person and iterations of that person' (Edberg 2004, 258). It therefore captures both the various meanings attached to being such a persona, and it offers a 'prototype for how to act those meanings in practice' (Edberg 2004). The question of what young migrants imagine they will become through migration is, of course, highly varied; however, as I show below, I observed a pattern in the narratives of prospective au pairs on Bohol, as well as among current and former au pairs, that expressed ideas about what I call an OFW persona – OFW being Overseas Filipino Worker. As I will show with the story of Rosemary below, this cultural persona is associated with positive achievements such as being knowledgeable about the world, living up to local standards of beauty, enjoying financial betterment and, as a result, becoming a person who can contribute financially to their home society and to family relations in particular. Aspirations to become such a persona should, however, also be understood in relation to the limited opportunities for social and economic mobility available within the Philippines for young, middle-class Filipinos today.

Rosemary,[4] for example, a 32-year-old former au pair, said that she had gone abroad to earn 'ok money'. However, this was not the only reason: 'my dream was to see the world, I wanted to see different countries, different people. I did not want to stop and say my life is like this. It's like stagnant water'. By comparing staying in the Philippines with 'stagnant water,' she was implying that she aspired to move 'up and out' in life. Surely, as for other au pairs, moving out was not a matter of adventure alone. The au pair's economic means (and passport status) simply do not allow for journeys with the sole purpose of adventure. Rather, prospective and current au pairs present their imaginings of travel within the framework of labour migration. Social ties to family and friends working in other countries feed this desire to migrate. One au pair explained, for example, that she began dreaming about going overseas when she saw pictures of the neighbour's daughter posing in fancy foreign clothes in front of a beautiful building abroad. Her dreams of migrating were not only based on a wish to help the family and to see the world. They were also grounded in the desire to become a person who was in a position to do these things – a person to look up to, like the neighbour's daughter with her experience of the wider world.

For Rosemary, the au pair stay became a stepping stone to permanent settlement abroad.[5] Initially she thought going to Denmark would serve as a way to move on to Norway and later Canada, but she became romantically involved with a Dane. The two married when Rosemary's au pair residence expired and she found work at a residential home in the Copenhagen area. In Danish society, she does not have a prestigious occupation; however, living and working in Europe increased her status back home. When I joined Rosemary on her vacation in her home village on Bohol in 2011, we received a warm welcome, and a steady flow of neighbours dropped by to greet her. Several also came to her with their problems: one had a rash on her arm and needed money for cream; another was out of shampoo, and yet another out of cigarettes. Rosemary willingly met their requests and, having saved up for almost 3 years for her visit, she even invited the whole neighbourhood for a feast.

Migrants such as Rosemary are clearly admired by local youths. When I asked some teenage girls about their future dreams, they answered with one voice that they wanted 'to become a success'. 'I want to go abroad', one of them elaborated. These girls did not talk directly about the financial gains migration brings, but rather about their aspirations to become 'a successful person'. Rosemary's presence in the village offered an example of what a stay abroad might lead to. She knew about life in Europe, and with her fashionable foreign clothes and pale skin, caused by the lack of sun in Scandinavia, she lived up to local ideas of beauty. However, to be admired at home, it was crucial that she help her neighbours and family. Local understandings of individual success thus not only involve personal gain but also the ability to contribute to the home society. As one au pair puts it: 'it's not worth anything for me if I just prioritize myself'. McKay (2012) has shown how the ability to meet the expectations of those at home is central to how Filipino migrants from the village of Haliap come to understand themselves as persons. I suggest that this observation applies to Filipino migrants more broadly. The transformation they achieve – or aspire to achieve – through migration therefore happens in relation to the meaning attached to becoming the persona embodied by the OFW. They practice and make visible this persona at the level of their re-positioning vis-à-vis friends and neighbours and within their own families.

Social re-positioning within the family: notions of maturity and independence

When au pairs and other young migrants re-position themselves at home by going abroad, their ability to contribute to the family economy is central. Being in a position to give, rather than in need of receiving, is embedded in local notions of independence and, according to current and former au pairs and their parents, becoming independent is one of the main things young Filipinas learn when they are in Denmark as au pairs. When the au pairs prioritise the needs of those receiving remittances, it also enables them to achieve a certain decision-making power within their families. Expectations concerning how to distribute resources are, however, contingent on local understandings of what it means to be mature; and it matters that the au pairs are unmarried women below 30 years of age. In the Boholano villages, married couples with children are perceived as adults who need to support their own family. They are therefore generally not obliged to help their parents financially. It is a different matter with unmarried men and especially unmarried women, who are still part of the parental household. As I show below with the story of Liane, by sending remittances home, young migrants are able to assert their position as adults who are able to make decisions concerning their own lives and the lives of those back home.

When Liane's au pair contract expired, she overstayed and became an undocumented immigrant working in Denmark. Like the other au pairs from her village, Liane would call home before sending her remittances. Liane's mother told how, during their last telephone conversation, Liane had first asked about the family's needs and then prioritised how the family was to spend the PhP 2900 (€54) she was sending: PhP 200 (€3.76) for each of Liane's siblings, another PhP 200 for her brother's imminent graduation and PhP 300 (€5.6) for his birthday present. Liane also asked her mother to buy her brother a birthday cake. The remaining money was at the mother's disposal. The mother used some money to feed the pigs and some to pay off the family's debts in various stores. The mother further related that the family had received bags of rice in return for money that Liane had lent to fellow villagers. The rice belonged to Liane but because of economic hardship, the family had begun eating it. They depended heavily on her help and I suggest that this dependence was central to the status she had achieved in her family. 'When she graduated from college, we said she was mature,' Liane's mother explained and added, 'but now she is abroad alone, she has really matured. Liane also says, "I am adult, I can decide"... she has her own ideas, she is independent'. Liane's mother went on to say that before she migrated, Liane was obedient and followed her parents' decisions. Referring to Liane's recent vacation at home, her mother said, 'before, if she wanted to go out and her father said no, she would stay [home]. Now she goes out if she wants, but she will still consult us'. Liane's mother thus saw her daughter's maturity as something that first developed through college, but then accelerated through migration. Exemplifying this with Liane's ability to ignore her parents' decisions (though she was still expected to consult them), the mother connected Liane's development with the independence she had acquired by being abroad alone.

It was a recurrent theme in the au pairs' (and their parents') narratives that migration was a way to become 'independent', as they termed it. The notion of independence is closely associated with perceptions of personal demarcation that vary cross-culturally. When I asked Gil, a former au pair in Denmark, how she understood independence, she explained, 'Being independent is I am supporting myself with my own money. I work hard, so if I want something I could buy it. I could do what I want'. Being independent, however, does not necessarily imply that the migrant is only responsible for herself. Gil, for example, supported both her parents and her two brothers, one of whom was attending college, which is a high expense. Rather than evoking an understanding of independence that implied autonomy, Gil described herself as an independent person as opposed to being a dependent, or what she called a 'standby'. Gil and other former au pairs from Bohol used this term to denote persons who, they explained, just stood around and waited for money.

Elsie, another former au pair, expressed a similar perception of independence when talking about an argument she had with her Filipino husband because he did not want her to have a job: 'I don't want to depend on anyone', Elsie explained. 'I want to depend on myself. I am used to that. That is the major thing I learned when I went abroad. I have to be independent. You have to stand on your own'. I suggest that when au pairs aspire to become independent through migration this is closely related to the ability to sustain themselves financially as well as to give financial support to family members, the first being a precondition for the latter. This entails responsibility and decision-making power, and it requires financial means as well as the willingness to balance one's own and other people's needs. Young people from Bohol emphasised the importance of prudence and unselfishness when describing their understanding of maturity and adulthood. Elsie explained that maturity is, 'how you think. If you think more – not just about yourself, if you think more of the future'. In a similar vein, Rosie, a young woman who had worked as a maid during her college studies, said that she 'grew up with her job'. Elaborating, 'I became an adult when I worked here [where she was maid], as I budgeted my money for important things, for my family'. When au pairs send money home it can therefore be seen as an enactment of maturity that demonstrates that they are contributing adult members of their families.

Being on one's own: freedom and social exclusion

Present and former au pairs and their parents did not view independence as something connoting only financial independence. In fact, several former au pairs (and their parents) emphasised that one thing they (or their children) had learned in Denmark was how to live without their parents. When asked what she had learned abroad, a former au pair answered: 'to stand on my own feet, to be independent, to decide on my own, to be strong – I was far from my loved ones, that is a big challenge'. This kind of independence, however, is not necessarily connected to the au pair stay but more generally to living on one's own for the first time. Referring to her first migration, leaving to work as a domestic in Manila, another former au pair explained that she left home because she wanted to 'improve herself' and to 'stand on her own', adding 'I don't want to depend all the time on my parents'. Gaining independence in this way is not seen as an easy task. Ana Lin, a former au pair I met on Bohol, recalled the difficulties she experienced moving at the age of 18 to work on the neighbouring island of Cebu: 'It was challenging because [...] everything that I do I have to live it on my own ... It is not easy to be alone'. Having 'to live everything on one's own' offers a sharp contrast to life at home, where adult children live in large families and are expected to consult and obey their parents. However, such nurture and protection goes hand-in-hand with control.

While the au pairs framed their move as challenging, some also emphasised that they found pleasure in escaping the watchful eyes at home. Due to parents' fear of pregnancies, the whereabouts of Filipina girls are often restricted. Such pregnancies are seen as shameful and expensive, and abortion is neither morally nor legally acceptable. In many cases, pregnancy out of wedlock means that a young female student must terminate her education and/or rush into marriage. Danish host families have a very different approach to such matters. Pre-marital sex is widely accepted in Danish society, and host families rarely consider protecting their au pairs from the dangers of Danish nightlife and romantic relations. As one au pair put it: 'it's like you've been jailed and off-jailed'. Another au pair similarly explained that one of the great things about going abroad was gaining freedom, having been restrained by parental control until she came to Denmark at the age of 24. She returned to this issue on several occasions, explaining that when she attended college in the Philippines she was frustrated about having a 6 PM curfew and being denied the opportunity to have a boyfriend or attend parties.

Village life, where members of the extended family often live close by and casually enter one another's homes throughout the day, offers a strong contrast to how au pairs experienced family life in Denmark. Au pairs and hosts rarely spend their leisure time together, and many au pairs participate only to a limited extent in the everyday life of their hosts. Some even claim that they feel 'pushed to become independent' by host parents who insist that they must learn to manage on their own. One example of this is when hosts expect a newly arrived au pair single-handedly to find her way to church, language school or the doctor's by public transport. Host families similarly explain that they encourage their au pairs to go about on their own, and some explicitly tell their au pairs that they do not expect them to spend their free evening with the host family. The host mothers that I interviewed recalled how they, when young, had preferred to live their social life quite separately from their own parents and elder generations and that they thought the au pairs should lead a similar life. Such views mirror Gullestad's observation that in Western societies individuality tends to be expressed by demarcating individual difference and distinction, as when youth 'resist and reshape the influence of parents' (Gullestad 1997, 215). It is an insistence on a form of independence that allows the hosts to limit the time and energy they invest in receiving a young foreigner into their home, which some au pairs perceived as a painful indifference on the part of the host family. Others, on the other hand, thought it enhanced the freedom they enjoyed.

Conclusions

The educational purpose of au pair placement, that is, that young people should develop themselves through a broadening of their cultural horizons, implies an understanding of personal development that, as has been argued in this article, varies cross culturally. Thus, the notion of a cultural persona embodied by Philippine migrants abroad influences the sort of personal development that young Filipinas seek through their au pair stay. The fact that such a personal transformation, to a great extent, is enabled by an improvement of their economic position and that they therefore have an economic incentive to migrate, does not preclude young Filipinas also seeing their au pair stay as a formative journey. So, the strong ambition to go abroad displayed by young people on Bohol should not be understood only in relation to the economic mobility that migration enables but also in relation to how migration can enable them to change, in particular, their social position in their home community in the Philippines and within their families. Remittances are a central means whereby the au pairs re-position themselves and become regarded as mature family members. From a Philippine vantage point, au pair migration can therefore be understood as a formative journey allowing young people to achieve recognition in their societies of origin because of their highly valued knowledge about the wider world and their ability to support those back home.

Such personal development is not necessarily unique for those engaging in the au pair scheme but could apply to young migrants more broadly. Other studies have shown that young people can use migration as a means to hasten their recognition as mature adults. Osella and Osella (2003), for example, show how young Keralese men, through migration, accelerated the progress 'along a culturally idealized trajectory towards mature manhood' (118). In this case, there was also a strong relationship between money and maturity, as the male migrants' ability to contribute financially to the home would give them recognition as being mature. Still, they needed to balance the way they used their financial capital because the ability to display wealth was also an important expression of masculinity. The Filipina au pairs balance their use of resources in a slightly different manner. Like the Keralese male migrants, engaging in consumption practices that contradict the expression of altruistic maturity and social involvement with those back home is also central to their ideas of personal success. As women, however, the au pairs are to a larger extent expected to remit to their natal home, because the sending of remittances to parents' households is a key aspect of gendered ideals of being good daughters or sisters. Through migration they thus acquire higher social status in their local society, which allows them to re-position themselves within their families, as long as they live up to the ideals of maturity, prudence, and independence that are associated with adulthood in Philippine society. Despite the many ambiguities, uncertainties, and possibilities of exploitation that are associated with au pairing, it is therefore regarded, in the au pairs' home communities, as an attractive pathway towards personal development for young women.

Acknowledgements

This work was supported by The Danish Council for Independent Research [10 080278]. I thank professor Karen Fog Olwig, Associate Professor Karen Valentin, Professor Claire Alexander and the four reviewers for their constructive comments.

Notes

1. 97% of the au pairs in Denmark are female (Liversage, Bille, and Jakobsen 2013, 92). I therefore employ the feminine Filipina hereafter.
2. Other au pairs may pay up to PhP 150.000 (€2726) in recruitment fees.
3. Prior to this opening, there are examples of young people from 'Western' countries, such as the United States, Australia who have been au pairs in Denmark.
4. Informants' names have been anonymised.
5. The number of people receiving family reunification with a spouse from the Philippines has grown parallel with the increase in the number of Filipina au pairs. In 2012, 210 Filipino citizens received residence through their Danish marriage partner (Grunnet and Binder 2014).

References

Aguilar, F. V. 1999. "Ritual Passage and the Reconstruction of Selfhood in International Labour Migration." *Journal of Social Issues in Southeast Asia* 14: 98 139. doi:10.1355/SJ14 1D.

Alipio, C. J. B. A. 2009. *Affective Economies: Child Debts, Devotions, and Desires in Philippine Migrant Families*. Washington, DC: University of Washington.

Anderson, B. 2007. "A Very Private Business. Exploring the Demand for Migrant Domestic Workers." *European Journal of Women's Studies* 14: 247 264. doi:10.1177/1350506807079013.

Asis, M. M. B. 2006. *The Philippines' Culture of Migration*. Migration Policy Institute. Accessed May 28, 2013. http://www.migrationpolicy.org/article/philippines culture migration

Bangko Sentral ng Pilipinas. 2014. "Overseas Filipinos' (OF) Remittances." Bangko Central ng Pilipinas. Accessed July 3. http://www.bsp.gov.ph/statistics/keystat/ofw.htm

Barber, P. G. 2004. "Contradictions of Class and Consumption When the Commodity Is Labour." *Anthropolossssgica* 46: 203 218. doi:10.2307/25606195.

Boer, F. 1987. "Nederlandse Meisjes in Parijs. Ontstaan En Ontwikkeling Van Het Au Pair Wezen in Frankrijk." Student Research Rapport. Universiteit van Amsterdam.

Brauer, J. G. C. 1959. *The Education of a Gentleman. Theories of Gentlemanly Education in England, 1660 1775*. New York: Bookman Associates.

Bulloch, H. 2009. "In Pursuit of Progress: Narratives of Transformation on a Philippine Island." Doctor of Philosophy, The Australian National University.

Commission on Filipinos Overseas. 2012a. *CFO to Conduct Country Familiarization Seminar for Europe Bound Au Pairs*. Manila: CFO. Accessed February 24, 2014. http://www.cfo.gov.ph/index.php?option com content&view article&id 1612:cfo to conduct country familiarization seminar for europe bound au pairs&catid 108: cfo press release&Itemid 839

Commission on Filipinos Overseas. 2012b. *Stock Estimate of Overseas Filipinos, as of December 2011*. Commission on Filipinos Overseas. Accessed March 5, 2014. http://www.cfo.gov.ph/images/stories/pdf/2011 Stock Estimate of Filipinos Overseas.pdf

Council of Europe. 1969. *European Agreement on "Au Pair" Placement*. Strasbourg: Council of Europe. Accessed April 31, 2014. http://conventions.coe.int/Treaty/en/Treaties/Html/068.htm

Edberg, M. 2004. "The Narcotrafficker in Representation and Practice: A Cultural Persona from the U.S. Mexican Border." *Ethos* 32: 257 277. doi:10.1525/eth.2004.32.2.257.

Gullestad, M. 1997. "Time for Children or Time for Adults?" In *Childhood Matters: Social Theory, Practice and Politics*, edited by J. E. A. Qvortrup. Aldershot: Avebury.

Grunnet, H., and M. Binder. 2014. *Tal og Fakta på Udlændingeområdet 2013*. Copenhagen: Udlændingestyrelsen.

Hess, S., and A. Puckhaber. 2004. "'Big Sisters' Are Better Domestic Servants?! Comments on the Booming Au Pair Business." *Feminist Review* 65 78. doi:10.1057/palgrave.fr.9400177.

Johnson, M., and P. Werbner. 2010. "Diasporic Encounters, Sacred Journeys: Ritual, Normativity and the Religious Imagination among International Asian Migrant Women." *The Asia Pacific Journal of Anthropology* 11: 205 218. doi:10.1080/14442213.2010.517510.

Larsen, B. 2004. *Au Pair Håndbogen*. København: Forlaget Pressto.

Liversage, A., R. Bille, and V. Jakobsen. 2013. *Den Danske Au Pair Ordning. En Kvalitativ Og Kvantitativ Undersøgelse*. Copenhagen: SFI Det nationale forsknings center for velfærd.

McKay, D. 2012. *Global Filipinos, Migrants' Lives in the Virtual Village*. Bloomington: Indiana University Press.

Mellini, L., C. Yodanis, and A. Godenzi. 2007. "'On Par'? The Role of the Au Pair in Switzerland and France." *European Societies* 9: 45 64. doi:10.1080/14616690601079432.

Osella, F. and C. Osella. 2003. "Migration, Money and Masculinity in Kerala." *Journal of the Royal Anthropological Institute* 6: 117 133. doi:10.1111/1467 9655.t01 1 00007.

Pratt, G. 2009. "Circulating Sadness: Witnessing Filipina Mothers' Stories of Family Separation." *Gender, Place & Culture* 16: 3 22. doi:10.1080/09663690802574753.

Rodriguez, R. M. 2010. *Migrants for Export. How the Philippine State Brokers Labor to the World*. Minneapolis: University of Minnesota Press.

Stenum, H. 2011. *Abused Domestic Workers in Europe: The Case of Au Pairs*. Brussels: European Parliament.

Yodanis, C., and S. R. Lauer. 2005. "Foreign Visitor, Exchange Student, or Family Member? A Study of Au Pair Policies in the United States, United Kingdom, and Australia." *International Journal of Sociology and Social Policy* 25: 41 64. doi:10.1108/01443330510791171.

Converting experiences in 'communities of practice': 'educational' migration in Denmark and achievements of Ukrainian agricultural apprentices

Vera Skvirskaja

This article looks at 'educational' migration instigated by the Danish pro gramme of agricultural apprenticeships, which since the late 1990s has brought many young Ukrainians to rural Denmark. It discusses discrepancies between the logic of achievement implied by the programme's ideology on the one hand, and Ukrainian apprentices' aspirations to social mobility on the other hand. In this way, the article questions the concept of 'community of practice' that has been used to describe the formation of a social persona sharing the values of this community. Using ethnographic case studies of former apprentices, I argue that while apprenticeships often fail to produce a shared social and professional identity within a community of practice, there are many ways in which the experiences afforded by Danish apprenticeships lead to (sometimes unforeseen) achievements.

Introduction

This article opens up a space for discussions of 'achievement' in the study of migration. It deals with agricultural apprenticeships undertaken by young Ukrainians in Denmark and with the discrepancy between the ideas of professional and/or social mobility that they ideologically stipulate and the subjective experiences of achievement that they practically facilitate. In recent writings in the Western mass media, apprenticeship as a hands-on way to gain skills and qualifications has been endorsed as an alternative to, or a complementary component of, a university degree. In a world dominated by 'the language of achievement' (Long and Moore 2013, 2), apprenticeship is routinely promoted as an authentic route to the top.[1] And it is commonly implied that 'reaching the top' happens within a 'community of practice' where apprenticeship is taking place (see. Lave and Wenger 1991).

In Denmark, apprenticeships are very common and available to both EU and non-EU citizens. The latter, such as Ukrainians, are subject to Danish migration regulations that stipulate that only people between the ages of 18 and 35 can obtain a work permit for a period of 18 months to undergo an apprenticeship that is professionally relevant for either their current or recently completed vocational or higher education in their home country. In Denmark, as in many other countries, the ideology of apprenticeship is about a humble, low-paid start leading to professional mobility or achievement within a specific, pre-defined sector. In Danish agriculture, this vision has historical roots that pre-date institutionally organised apprenticeships: farmers' sons and daughters were traditionally expected to gain experience away from home on farms of similar or larger size than their parents' for paltry wages (Fabricius 1996, 77–80).

Since the late 1990s, the number of Danish apprentices has fallen sharply and Danish farmers have come to rely on apprentices from former socialist countries (Larsen 2010, 91), particularly Ukraine.[2] There are myriad recruiters and Internet sites that offer to match Ukrainian men and women (both genders are in demand) to Danish farmers. In contrast to apprentices from EU countries, Ukrainians' geographic mobility is more constrained and their migration costs are higher (visas, fake diplomas, etc.) and all this makes them a more dependable and therefore reliable labour force.

The Danish apprenticeship scheme can serve as an example of a highly structured migration route (see Sassen 1999, 2) crafted by Danish policy makers. The inflow of new migrants from Eastern Europe that it facilitates has, however, provoked some discontent in Danish society. Trade unions are concerned with social dumping: the number of young Danes interested in agriculture had certainly fallen,[3] but farmers, it is argued, are saving on their expenses and offer scant training to foreigners.[4] Danish experts on human trafficking have likewise identified apprentices from Eastern Europe as a 'vulnerable group' (Lisborg 2011, 87) subject to forms of exploitation such as excessive fees charged by recruiters, unpaid overtime, poor living conditions and no remuneration of certain services (e.g. cleaning, home repairs). The migration context of foreign apprentices only serves to highlight what Herzfeld (2003, 4) noted in his discussion of Greek artisan apprentices – that is, the practices of apprenticeship illuminate aspects of inequality that employers and workers in other arrangements and other parts of the world are better positioned to conceal.

Ukrainian apprentices have also come under public scrutiny for a different reason. Many have been coming to Denmark with 'fake' university/college papers that qualify them for apprenticeship and so have violated the Danish migration regime. Apropos of this issue, the Danish minister of employment stated that society 'should be ready to be open to foreign students but only to those who have the right to be here' (see Borg 2012). From the perspective of supposed illegality and job competition, Ukrainians, just as generations of migrant labourers in Europe before them, are seen as undesirable 'others' in wider society (Sassen 1999, 134–35). Even though farmers take Ukrainian apprentices without scruples regarding the authenticity of their degrees, what matters is that they get a hardworking reliable workforce at a discount rate (see Note 4) – 'fake' apprentices are described in the Danish press as people 'who cheated their way into Danish jobs' (Borg 2012).

Many scholars, in turn, discuss apprenticeships as a form of education that not only teaches technical skills but also provides a basis for personal formation, such as 'worldviews and moral principles' (Marchand 2008, 246) or that represents 'an embodied project of self making through the acquisition ... of expertise' (Prentice 2012, 409). Lave and Wenger's (1991) notion of 'communities of practice', with its developmental cycle wherein a newcomer gradually acquires the identity of a full practitioner or a proper member, has a good deal of currency in this field of study.

The aim of this article is to explore Ukrainian apprentices' conceptualisations of 'achievement', the social personae produced by apprenticeships and what this can tell us about 'communities of practice' in all actuality. I do not intend to analyse the pedagogical context of apprenticeships; instead, my ethnographic focus here is on individual life-trajectories and stories of achievement. Contrary to the scholarly perspectives mentioned above, these stories show that an apprenticeship on a Danish farm does not necessarily contribute to the production of a shared professional identity or a common sense of solidarity characteristic of a community of practice. They illustrate that the ideology of apprenticeship may or may not cohere with feelings of achievement that emerge, as Long and Moore (2013) point out, 'through affective and evaluative engagement with things that have to be done in the world' (2013, 3).

Methodological considerations: 'event' and 'achievement'

The ethnographic data for this article comes primarily from socialising with former apprentices at their homes or in public places, both in Denmark (Vejle and Copenhagen) and Ukraine (Kiev, Zhitomir, Uman, Lviv and Odessa). I interviewed and periodically met up with approximately 15 former apprentices. My interlocutors were both men and women,[5] including husbands and wives who were apprenticed together. While some had just completed their apprenticeships when we met, others had done so several years earlier.[6] Talking to people who have completed their apprenticeships and moved on allowed for some biographical depth, reflecting changing motivations and revealing the diversity of life trajectories, from a seasonal migrant labourer to an accountant in a multinational consultancy firm. To get a feel for people's work and social environment in Denmark, I also visited several farms in Jutland.

Following leads provided by former apprentices, we can view apprenticeship as initiating a 'movement between two worlds' (Sassen 1999, 135) and as a cross-border experience marked by the asymmetry of cross-cultural encounters (Bacas and Kavanagh 2013). For many (but not all), Danish apprenticeship was their first visit to Western Europe and constituted an 'event' because it actualised ideas people held about their identity – what it means to be 'myself', to be a particular person. Even though it might not have been an event that entailed a radical rupture of previous knowledge(s) (Humphrey 2008), it was an event that had the potential for opening up new horizons and fields of creativity.

In selecting case studies of apprentices' life trajectories that I will discuss towards the end of this paper, I have used the criterion of apprenticeship as an event, leading to subjectively felt and socially recognised achievement. Of course, this approach is not free from methodological pitfalls. On the one hand, there are variations in people's understandings of achievement and the significance of achievement may rapidly fade with time, especially in broadly speaking unfavourable circumstances. On the other hand, just like an event that may be acclaimed by some people but not others around them (Humphrey 2008, 363), achievement is a relational idea. In documenting 'achievement', I endeavour to reflect the considerations of my interlocutors, both men and women, who were less concerned with the money that they could save from their modest apprenticeship salaries (and what this money could buy) and were more focused on attaining a good life and a 'real future'.

Let me give the example of a Ukrainian couple in their late twenties whose outcome of apprenticeship is very common and does not illustrate achievement along the lines suggested here. Elena and Mikhail returned to their hometown in Ukraine at the end of their Danish apprenticeship and invested their savings in a new flat. When I met Elena, two years after she had left Denmark, she was reading for a PhD in horticulture, while her husband was a construction worker in Russia and rarely visited home. Elena's PhD provided her with a small stipend. She did not envisage an academic career; her thoughts were on new migration – anywhere at all, but *with* her husband. 'At least on the farm we had a life together', she said, emphasising the key aspect of her agricultural apprenticeship. There was no strong sense of achievement related to her Danish experience; even the flat seemed somehow 'devalued' – this once desirable object now anchored them to a place where they could no longer live together.

What Elena's (and Mikhail's) story illustrates nicely is that the ability to buy a new car or a new flat as a result of a Danish apprenticeship may not be sufficient to have a profound positive impact on an individual life-trajectory or on social standing. So, the selected cases illustrate not the typical 'achievements' of Ukrainian apprentices or the achievements of 'typical' apprentices, but the ways in which 'achievement' is realised as social-professional mobility and is the outcome of individual intentions or planning (to 'achieve'). The controversial and often unintended role played by Danish agricultural apprenticeships in this kind of achievement will become more comprehensible if we first consider the overall educational context in Ukraine.

Education in Ukraine: from 'gift' to 'commodity'

Examination of the current situation in Ukrainian higher education reveals the almost impossible nature of Danish migration requirements for agricultural apprentices, as well as underscoring the fact that opportunism is the main available strategy for most young Ukrainians. The issue at stake is the blurred categories of 'fake' and 'authentic' degrees. No less important are the formal structures of college degrees and fees. Let us look at these two issues in turn.

The Ukrainian higher education sector, many Ukrainians believe, delivers scant opportunities for professional mobility. If in Soviet times, education was a 'gift' from the socialist state, nowadays, it is a 'commodity' in a dual sense. First, it is a commodity because students can 'buy' good exam results (sometimes, they have to pay for good marks even when their performance warrants them). Sergei, a graduate of an agricultural university, recounted: 'In essence, our studies are a joke. During the first meeting with students, a teacher introduces himself: "hello, my name is so and so, let's collect some money from you guys now because it is only going to be more expensive later"'. Corruption in the educational sphere is common knowledge and many degrees are no longer recognised in countries that used during the Soviet period to train their specialists in Ukraine (e.g. Egypt, Turkey, Iran).[7]

Second, education is a commodity because it is not free for all – the state sets aside quotas of free places, reflecting the state's demand for particular professions. These quotas are filled by the best school graduates, called *biudgetniki* in Russian (i.e. 'on the state budget'), who are also entitled to a stipend. All other students, called *kontraktniki* ('on contracts'), have to pay fees. Official fees for education or 'the contract' are correlated with the 'prestige' of the subject and the university. A contract with the department of economics at the agricultural university is, for instance, cheaper than a contract with a department of economics at a state university. As a result, poorer families can only afford the least prestigious and cheapest colleges and university departments. Rather than being an individual achievement, education has largely become a token of one's family's material standing – what kind of degree you can afford to *buy* – creating structures of distinction just like the consumption of any other commodity (see Bourdieu 1984).

This system of 'contracts' and 'budget places' has important implications for students who consider undertaking agricultural apprenticeships in Denmark. It is the very category of people defined by Danish authorities as the 'right' candidates for an apprenticeship that is worst positioned to participate in the programme. Agricultural universities are mainly popular with youths from the countryside and small towns, who can only attend university if they receive a free place. But free higher education presupposes the observance of certain rules. An 18-month long apprenticeship in Denmark is not considered as an acceptable reason for a student to take academic leave (*akademotpusk*, Russian). A student who takes an 18-month long apprenticeship has two options – either to interrupt his/her studies to go to Denmark and then, upon return, resume these studies as a fee-paying student, '*kontraktnik*', or to bribe his/her way back to a free place, which may not always be feasible.

To summarise, the Danish requirements for apprentices from outside the EU, which emphasise professional mobility within a single industry, do not take into account the *de facto* and *de jure* situation of Ukrainian students. A distinction between 'fake' and 'authentic' university papers is often meaningless. The very difference between 'authentic' apprentices and the rest only regards the 'spirit of the rules', not actual practice: some people enter agricultural colleges on a contract basis and pay for their exams only in order to receive all the necessary documentation from the college to qualify for a Danish apprenticeship. There are various schemes in operation. I met Ukrainian recruiters who require candidates to work for food only on their private farms in order to equip them with papers certifying that they have had relevant agricultural training. A small point I want to make here is that given that Ukrainian degrees have largely been reduced to commodities in free circulation (independent of knowledge acquisition), the division of apprentices in Denmark into 'fake' and 'authentic' tells us little about the role of apprenticeships in people's professional and social mobility.

Making a move

The issue of achievement is pertinent for many apprentices because they have encountered, or are aware of, the stigma associated with cheap manual labour abroad. Several of my informants recalled that family members and strangers were scornful of their decision to become agricultural apprentices: 'You do not study foreign languages or plant ecology to end up cleaning pigsties somewhere in Denmark!' Whatever the rhetoric of recruiters may be (and they habitually emphasise the experience of work abroad, improved command of English and the possibility of subsequent employment abroad),[8] few Ukrainians would seriously consider agricultural apprenticeships to be 'educational migration'.[9]

Apprentices come from different regions of Ukraine (the majority are from the more economically deprived areas), but they share a similar social background. Most of them come from small provincial towns and villages, from lower-, middle- and working-class families whose familiarity with agriculture, where it exists, amounts mainly to tending the pigs or a cow kept in the backyard of their grandmother's house. Many have studied or lived in big cities, where they are called 'incomers' (*priezzhie*, Russian). Nikolai, who ended up living in Copenhagen, reflected upon his own provincialism. In 2005, he arrived in the provincial Danish city of Aalborg in Jutland: 'Aalborg was my first city in Denmark, well, in Europe! It was a revelation – it was exactly how I had imagined Western Europe! The main shopping street – it was like Las Vegas!'

For most of these young 'provincials', 'earning money' or escaping from a situation where there is little hope that anything will ever change for the better – is the main motivation for going to Denmark, at least initially. As Andrei, a graduate of a Foreign Languages University who came to Denmark in 2005 and continued to work on Danish farms when his apprenticeship expired, recalled: 'When you arrive, you are given a spade... They explain ad hoc what is "interesting" for us to know, but we are interested in how to make money. Nobody was really interested in going into the details.' Young people usually earmark their earnings for themselves, including their partners and children; cash remittances to kin are rare.

Although 'earning money' is declared to be the primary goal, over the course of our conversations, it also became clear that in Denmark new ideas and opportunities could and sometimes did present themselves. For many, the act of migration – an 'event' – held out the promise of exploration of unknown realms, including oneself and one's own capacities for action. Danish experiences coupled with different expectations of achievement, led people to a variety of professional careers and business ventures. Below, I provide some background to Danish apprenticeships and then discuss how Danish experiences were deployed in the post-apprenticeship lives of some of my interlocutors.

'Educational migration'

Transmission of knowledge

A fundamental characteristic of any apprenticeship is that it is a practice of learning embedded in a work environment. The ideal of the modern Danish farm is 'the efficient farmer' and not 'Danish family farming' (*familiebrug*, Danish). The proprietor of a farm works physically on his farm with a single helper or a couple of helpers for most of the time. His wife often has a job outside the farm while children attend nurseries and kindergartens. Even though 'he identifies with the production', the contemporary farmer is also akin to a company director in charge of expensive equipment (Fabricius 1996, 126–131). Whatever the common current 'farmer template' may be, Ukrainian apprentices end up on a range of differently organised and staffed farms. Some are small farms with few or no outside workers. Others are large estates consisting of different farms where the farmer does not do physical work, but employs a number of Danish and foreign managers, workers and apprentices, and is rarely seen on the farm's subdivisions.

Depending on the type and size of the farm, the 'transmission of knowledge' takes different forms. On very small farms, a newcomer is usually introduced to his/her sphere of responsibilities by the farmer himself. On larger farms, farmers tend to rely on other Ukrainian or Russian-speaking workers (e.g. from the Baltic countries) to explain tasks to novices. As Oleg recalled: 'The first months I did not talk to my farmer. I dealt only with those Ukrainians who arrived before me. Much later, when I had to teach newcomers myself, the farmer would ask me about my plans for the day.'

There are very few written instructions available to new arrivals. A farmer or his manager expects an apprentice to remember procedures and Ukrainian old-timers who introduce farms to the novices tend to illustrate the way things should be done using short narratives. Oleg gave me an example: 'When you go to slaughter, you have to remember to put the shoes with metal tips on. Now, so-and-so did not put these shoes on, and look what happened to him.' Some apprentices, however, appreciate clear written instructions. Andrei broke with the oral 'tradition' and wrote a detailed list of instructions for new apprentices that he then laminated so that it would last longer. 'They are still using my list. That is a better way of explaining the farm,' he told me proudly back in Ukraine.

A farmer expects an apprentice to perform all his tasks unaided after a period of approximately three months. As one farmer told me, an apprentice is either 'capable' (*dygtig*, Danish) or 'not capable' (*ikke dygtig*). Instead of providing lengthy explanations, young people are encouraged to 'use their heads' (*bruge hovedet*, Danish). Farmers' emphasis on 'capableness' brings to the fore cultural continuity: 'capableness' (*dygtighed*) in agricultural matters has traditionally encapsulated the ideal of the Danish farmer, the highest grounds for respect, overriding 'human' qualities (Fabricius 1996, 73). My Ukrainian interlocutors explained that the problem is often not their 'capableness' as such, but has to do with the necessity to adjust to conditions and tasks on farms, which can range from the 'stench' (*von'*, Russian) to jobs considered 'revolting' (e.g. castration or killing of animals). 'When my farmer was told that I was avoiding killing sick pigs, he took me to slaughter, asked everybody to leave and told me to kill all the animals there myself,' Oleg recalled. '…I was killing those pigs until late at night… Sometimes I could not kill them properly and just made them suffer. It was awful'.

Those who cannot cope with the farm environment may choose to terminate their apprenticeships after a short period, even though it entails losing their investment in migration to Denmark. But there are also many more 'capable' apprentices who manage their tasks well and yet, do not consider themselves as belonging, in any way, to the community of practice represented by the Danish farming community.

Communities of practice

Anthropological analyses of apprenticeships often foreground the idea that apprenticeship is about building a social persona (see Herzfeld 2003; Marchand 2008). Lave and Wenger (1991) have argued that an important role in this process is played by the community of practice, which holds social values and attitudes pertaining to a particular profession. This process is not only circumscribed by the work place. The fostering of social ties and socialisation into a profession are equally crucial to the process of learning. In his study of Chinese potters, for instance, Gowlland (2012, 364) noted that everyday activities such as walking, cycling, driving to the workshops or homes of colleagues are opportunities to exchange information.

In the case of many Ukrainian apprentices, it is precisely this sociality, this way of 'fostering of ties' that rarely happens. Even the Danish farmers' 'use your head' approach sometimes provokes discontent because people are used to a very different style of learning: 'An apprentice is not a slave who came to you from abroad, he is a person who has to be taught'. This discontent echoes a common theme of apprentices' experiences 'that no one wants to teach them anything anyway' (Herzfeld 2003, 51), but Ukrainians' awareness of the power hierarchy at play (i.e. rich Western Europeans vs. poor Eastern Europeans) contributes to greater social distancing.

The 'transmission of knowledge' that follows 'national' or linguistic lines often facilitates divisions in the community of practice: an apprentice's growing familiarity with the practices of other Ukrainians includes strategies to keep Danish farmers 'in check' – from reporting abuses to local newspapers to keeping records of unpaid overtime and appealing to the trade unions. At an even more basic level, it seems that the practices of sociality and cultural values of the farming community prevent many Ukrainians from developing a sense of solidarity with or belonging to this 'community of practice'.

Some end up living in 'little Ukraines', to borrow Oleg's phrase, represented by the predominantly Ukrainian work collective of their farms, and maintain minimal contacts with Danish society. Many consider themselves lucky to have an apprenticeship 'in a little Ukraine' for social, practical and psychological reasons, and manage to spend their time in Denmark without mastering either English or Danish. Many also establish geographically extended networks with other Ukrainians, former Soviets and Eastern Europeans. The geographical dispersal of Ukrainian apprentices has not hampered an inward-looking diasporic sociality – social media such as Facebook and *Odnoklassniki* ('Classmates' in Russian) with its many groups made by and for migrants in Denmark are effective tools for gossip, searching for jobs and learning about situations on different farms.

Sociality with Danish colleagues can pose a problem in its own right. Some farmers who regularly host Ukrainians require their Danish workers to speak some English. Yet, even this well-meaning intention fails as workers may share the same table over lunch, but not engage in much 'cross-cultural' interaction. 'They laugh at their jokes. We discuss our matters. It is all friendly; we do not understand each other', Andrei recalled. Very few apprentices choose to pay extra to have meals with the farmer's family – an option offered by the apprenticeship programme in order to encourage the cultural immersion of Ukrainians – and at least one reason for this is the conflicting expectations of the parties involved. One Danish farmer complained to me that the weekly supplies for lunch he used to buy for his Ukrainian apprentices would disappear in a couple of days. The farmer saw this as an attempt by Ukrainians to profit from the arrangement by consuming more food than they were paying for. When I recounted this episode to my Ukrainian interlocutors who worked at different farms, their reaction was uniform – 'the farmer was stingy'; young Ukrainians preferred not to eat with their hosts or even drink 'their' coffee in order to avoid humiliating reproaches about 'excessive consumption of food'. Ukrainians interpret the limitations on consumption of food as farmers' inability to appreciate their hard work. 'We need lots of food because of the hard physical labour, and we make money for the farmer.'

There were also certain values held dear in the Danish farming community that my interlocutors were not willing to share. Historically, from the early twentieth century, Danish smallholders and estate cottagers were known for a combination of Spartan conduct in their everyday life and savings in the bank. Those agricultural labourers who were into quick spending, feasting and drinking enjoyed greater outward mobility but lacked security and tended to end up as a rural proletariat (Christiansen 1996, 419–423, 523–528). It is the thrifty Spartan type of farmer who strikes a discordant note with many Ukrainians, for whom achievement is about personal 'development' (*razvitie*, Russian) with all the benefits this may bring (e.g. a better-paid job, greater spending power). Oleg's comments were typical: 'I do not understand their life-philosophy. They work hard every day and economise on themselves. And the result of all this hard labour – they are dead at 70, with a million in the bank, but having lived a sad life...' This understanding of what it means to be a Danish farmer (or any farmer) is not surprising given that many Ukrainian apprentices come from a very different social background, as mentioned above, and entertain different ideals of upward mobility, as we shall see below.

Achievement – a biographical approach

Ukrainian apprentices on Danish farms presents us with a picture of the community of practice that is ridden with internal divisions and the absence of certain shared core values. Many former apprentices have secured work contracts in Denmark and many of those never had any agricultural education back in Ukraine. As one such worker told me: 'It is much easier to teach a graduate of a Foreign Languages University how to handle pigs than to teach a village bumpkin from an agricultural college how to speak English or Danish'. Herzfeld's (2003, 51) observation that what the apprentices learn 'has more to do with survival in an often adversarial social environment than with the acquisition of specific craft techniques' holds for Ukrainian apprentices. The main difference is that in the Greek case described by Herzfeld, apprenticeship is a training in the mastery of cultural intimacy where masters and apprentices come from the same social (under)class (2003, 22) while for Ukrainians striving to 'achieve', the issue at stake is the mastery of transnational intimacy and new competencies that they hope will propel them far above their 'masters' and the latters' community of practice.

There are of course many, like Elena and Mikhail mentioned in the introduction, for whom the 18-month long apprenticeship has led nowhere career-wise and has not produced a lasting sense of achievement. But, here I would like to consider the ways apprenticeship has initiated a new turn and/or vision in life that is clearly understood as achievement. I now proceed to look at three life trajectories that illustrate, however schematically, this diversity of achievement and production of new social personae. They are cases of particular personalities and experiences resulting from apprenticeship and migration to Denmark at a particular time.

Case 1. A shift in social identity

Mikhail was my only informant who proudly adopted the social identity of a 'full practitioner' in the agricultural community of practice. Originally from a poor village family, he studied at an Institute of Foreign Languages in a small town where he also worked at a recruitment company as an English tutor for agricultural apprentices planning to go to Denmark and the US. After graduating in 1998, Mikhail did not want to go back to his village to be a schoolteacher. 'I wanted to develop further', he told me. Unable to make ends meet, he eventually asked his employer to send him as an apprentice to Denmark.

Mikhail approached his apprenticeship stoically, 'like military service'. His farmer had a bad reputation among Ukrainians: he hardly spoke any English or German, he refused to pay overtime and never praised his workers. Mikhail did not despair and in a short while he could speak Danish with his farmer. He boarded with the farmer's family despite disliking the food he had to pay for ('they did not serve bread and had porridge for breakfast!') because he was interested in all aspects of the farmer's life. After Denmark, Mikhail spent a year on a farm in Ireland – 'a resort compared to Denmark' – and then resumed working for the recruiter teaching English.

In 2001, he met a Dane who was looking for a manager for his Ukrainian farm and got the job. The next seven years Mikhail spent on the Danish-owned farm with some twenty-five people working under him. When the farm was sold to new owners, in the wake of the financial crisis, Mikhail got a job at the Ministry of Agriculture as an analyst. It was a poorly paid job, but he became well known in farming business circles and in 2010 he was offered a managerial position at an international company comprising several large farms in Ukraine. Today, he is in charge of some seventy people and takes pride in his professional trajectory and new social identity: 'If favourable conditions are secured, I can be among the top five farmers in Ukraine. Now I am somebody here. ... That Danish farmer was a tough one, but it was a very good school (*klassnaia shkola*, Russian).'

Case 2. A pragmatic approach

I met Alex in Lviv where he was on a business trip. Because of his busy schedule, it was easier to catch up with him in Lviv than in Kiev where he is based at the national headquarters of a major international accounting firm. Alex studied accounting at an agrarian college located in his hometown and his ambition was to become an auditor at a big international firm, but his chances as a graduate of a provincial college were slim. Alex understood that he would need good English and experience of 'dealing' with foreigners to compete for his dream job. A Danish apprenticeship seemed a step in the right direction and after completing his BA, he spent 2007–2009 in a farm. Alex accepted the hard work as a given, enrolled in a Danish language school and also worked on the farmer's construction site to make some extra cash.

He spent his earnings on a car and covering migration expenses. 'Money issues' did not feature in his narrative. Instead, he emphasised that his Danish apprenticeship helped him to achieve his goal. Upon his return, he completed a Master's course in accounting while working as a full-time accountant at a Greek-owned factory – he got this job because he could freely converse in English with the Greek boss. Just a year later, he secured a job with an international accountancy firm. Everything played a role in this achievement – his good knowledge of English, basic Danish, his experience of living and working abroad and even his 'farming' credentials because the company also conducts audits of agricultural enterprises. 'There is a connection between my apprenticeship and my current work. To put it crudely, on the farm I worked on the "inside" and now I am dealing [with this business] from the "outside"'.

Case 3. Entrepreneurial ambitions

Anton liked to stress that his only reason for going to Denmark in 2002 was to earn money. With two 'useless' higher education degrees – in pedagogy and 'protection of flora', both from Kiev Agrarian University – he 'ran away from poverty'. Sipping tea in a fancy cafe in downtown Kiev, his phone constantly ringing, Anton reminisced about the four years spent on a Danish farm (at the end of his apprenticeship, he got a work contract). Moreover, Anton found other ways of making money – an 'illegal' business he would not describe to me and assembling computers from parts found at recycling stations. These activities, rather than the apprenticeship wages, allowed him to save up enough money to buy a small flat in Kiev. He also gained enough confidence to quit his Danish job and go back to Ukraine.

In the long term, Anton wanted to see himself as 'an independent man' and he saw no possibility of 'development' in farm work-cum-way-of-life. 'You are stuck with the animals, you have to love them... and a villager is a narrow-minded person – ... he cannot imagine living his life differently. Most Danish farmers are also narrow-minded...They do not explore new horizons (*perspek tivy*, Russian) in life'. Being a 'swineherd' in Denmark, as he called it, allowed Anton to achieve a life he wanted. He got a flat and a financial boost to start his own transportation firm. Although he insisted that his time in Denmark was only about making money, he also acknowledged that the idea of starting a transport business did not come from nowhere: 'Something pushed me to do this. People have to go to Denmark somehow, do they not? You could fly, but there was nothing else at the time.' Today Anton has eight mini buses and twelve trucks, and as competition on the Danish–Ukrainian routes gets tougher, Anton puts more effort into exporting second-hand Danish cars to Ukraine. New migration is considered a last resort only, as it is associated with his experience of farm life – useful but demeaning: 'Abroad, we will always remain in the position of swineherd and do hard manual labour.' Anton does not stay in touch with his Danish farmer, but now and then he sends him a box of chocolates with one of his minibuses.

Conclusion: a 'route to the top'?

Theorising from a focus on individual 'personalities' has often been part and parcel of the anthropological contribution to wider knowledge (see Jackson 2008; Humphrey 2008; Tsing 1993). As Jackson (2008, 70) points out in his tale of a Sierra Leonean migrant in London, much always depends upon an individual's inner resources as well as the values that have been instilled in him or her. In the case studies discussed above, I have attempted to show that there are myriad ways, depending on people's circumstances, but even more so on their person-alities and values, in which an apprenticeship can 'equip young people to operate more generally in the larger society of which they are members' (Herzfeld 2003, 50).

The present-day experience of vocational and higher education in Ukraine as an (opportunistic) commodity often fails to secure satisfactory careers for the provincial youths who make up the bulk of agricultural apprentices in Denmark. While an agricultural apprenticeship abroad does not enhance one's social status *per se* or improve professional mobility back home, for at least some young Ukrainians it is 'an event' that can provide them with an opportunity to (re-) assess or realise their aspirations, ambitions and capabilities, although this may have little to do with their life and work on the Danish farms. For people like Mikhail, Anton or Alex, the Danish apprenticeship itself proved to be an opportunity to 'achieve' – that is to become 'somebody', a social persona whom one can respect.

Following experiences of achievement of former Ukrainian apprentices (including their ideas about what kind of people they would like to be), I suggest that we need to rethink certain parameters of the idea of 'community of practice' where practice-based learning takes place. There are, of course, communities of practice where, as Lave and Wenger (1991) argue, novices forge an identity compatible with that of the group in order to be eventually accepted as full members of that group. And this is the ideology that underlies the Danish state's criteria of entitlement to agricultural apprenticeships in Denmark: compatibility with the group is warranted by one's identity, which has been developed over the course of one's education and professional orientation. Yet, as the diverse career routes and aspirations of former Ukrainian apprentices demonstrate, a straightforward professional trajectory starting with one's education and ending in a field circumscribed by this education does not necessarily constitute an achievement for many young people; it may be neither feasible nor desirable.

Instead, an apprenticeship in one kind of community of practice (in this case, 'farming') can also be used strategically to achieve greater mobility – both outward and upward – by shifting to a very different occupation. In the transnational realm of 'educational migration' represented by Danish agricultural apprenticeships, there are both conflations and confrontations of ideology and practice; while some apprentices adopted a social identity offered by 'the community', others fiercely resisted it, but to the extent that the experiences afforded by migration to Denmark have boosted the social and professional mobility of both 'fake' and 'authentic' apprentices, Danish apprenticeships have produced achievement in their own right.

Funding

This work was supported by the Danish Council for Independent Research in Humanities, [grant number 10 080278].

Notes

1. 'Apprenticeships to be the "new norm", says David Cameron'. 11 March 2013. www.bbc.co.uk/news/uk 21734560.
2. In the early 2000s, there were 500 700 Ukrainian apprentices arriving every year; their number rose to 2400 in 2007 08 and this figure had then halved by 2011. Source: Statistics from Danish Agency for Labour Retention and International Recruitment.
3. From 1996 to 2000, the number of Danish pupils at Danish agricultural schools required to undergo 18 months of apprenticeship had fallen by 40%. In 2005, two foreign farm apprentices were employed for each Danish one (Larsen 2010, 91).
4. http://www.ugebreveta4.dk/2005/10/Baggrundoganalyse/Landbrugetforetraekkerosteu ropaeiskarbejdkraft.aspx. Accessed 8 June 2013. Formal conditions of apprenticeship are the same for both EU and non EU citizens: a 37 hour working week and monthly net cash payments of around 6.500 7.0000 Danish krones.
5. I personally talked to three female apprentices, but learned about many others.
6. Insights into Ukrainian apprentices' experiences have also been gained from social media sites (e.g. Facebook and chat rooms).
7. I was told about this by my Turkish, Egyptian, Iranian and Syrian informants, as well as colleagues from different universities in Odessa in 2005 2013. See also, Osipian (2007), and 'Iran rejects Ukrainian medical universities' diplomas' (2011).
8. Promotional material disseminated by Odessa Agricultural University, March 2013, by the recruiter Tarasiuk S.V. from the Zhitomir region, Ukraine.
9. Ukrainian recruiters are required by Ukrainian law to have a special licence to employ people abroad and agricultural apprenticeships in Denmark are defined as 'work abroad'. There are multiple ways around this requirement, from 'illegal' (i.e. unli censed) practices to recruitment via organisations like a 'youth trade union' and international volunteer organisations'.

References

Bacas, J. L., and W. Kavanagh. 2013. "Introduction." In *Border Encountes. Asymmetry and Proximity at Europe's Frontiers*, edited by J. L. Bacas, and W. Kavangh, 1 24. New York: Berghahn.

Borg, O. 2012. "70 Ukrainere Har Snydt Sig Til Danske Job." *Jyllands-Posten*. Accessed December 2. http://jyllands-posten.dk/indland/article4931563.ece.

Bourdieu, P. 1984. *Distinction: A Social Critique of the Judgment of Taste*. London: Routledge.

Christiansen, P. O. 1996. *A Manorial World. Lord, Peasants and Cultural Distinctions on a Danish Estate 1750–1980*. Copenhagen: Scandinavian University Press.

Fabricius, N. 1996. *Landet Med de Store Gårde*. Haderslev: Landbohistorisk Selskab.

Gowlland, G. 2012. "Learning Craft Skills in China: Apprenticeship and Social Capital in an Artisan Community of Practice." *Anthropology and Education Quarterly* 43 (4): 358–371. doi:10.1111/j.1548-1492.2012.01190.x.

Herzfeld, M. 2003. *The Body Impolitic. Artisans and Artifice in the Global Hierarchy of Value*. Chicago, IL: The University of Chicago Press.

Humphrey, C. 2008. "Reassembling Individual Subjects: Events and Decisions in Troubled Times." *Anthropological Theory* 8 (4): 357–380. doi:10.1177/1463499608096644.

"Iran Rejects Ukrainian Medical Universities' Diplomas." 2011. *Kyiv Post*, June 11. http://www.kyivpost.com/content/business/iran-rejects-ukrainian-medical-universities-diplom-108417.html.

Jackson, M. 2008. "The Shock of the New: On Migrant Imaginaries and Critical Transitions." *Ethnos: Journal of Anthropology* 73 (1): 57–72. doi:10.1080/00141840801927533.

Larsen, M. 2010. "'Now I Sleep Good at Night' Østarbejdere I Dansk Landbrug." In *Årbog Arbejdermuseet*, edited by A. E. Hansen, 84–94. Copenhagen: Arbejdermuseet.

Lave, J., and E. Wenger. 1991. *Situated Learning. Legitimate Peripheral Participation*. Cambridge: Cambridge University Press.

Lisborg, A. 2011. *Menneskehandel I Den Grønne Sektor?* Odense: Servicestyrelsen, Center mod Menneskehandel.

Long, N. J., and H. Moore, eds. 2013. "Introduction: Achievement and Its Social Life." In *The Social Life of Achievement*, 1–30. New York: Berghahn.

Marchand, T. H. J. 2008. "Muscles, Morals and Mind: Craft Apprenticeship and the Formation of Person." *British Journal of Educational Studies* 56 (3): 245–271. doi:10.1111/j.1467-8527.2008.00407.x.

Osipian, A. 2007. "Higher education corruption in Ukraine as reflected in the nation's Media." MPRA Paper No. 8464. Accessed October 25, 2013. http://mpra.ub.uni-muenchen.de/8464/1/MPRA_paper_8464.pdf.

Prentice, R. 2012. "'No One Ever Showed Me Nothing': Skill and Self-Making among Trinidadian Garment Workers." *Anthropology and Education Quarterly* 43 (4): 400–414. doi:10.1111/j.1548-1492.2012.01193.x.

Sassen, S. 1999. *Guests and Aliens*. New York: The New Press.

Tsing, A. L. 1993. *In the Realm of the Diamond Queen: Marginality in an Out-Of-The-Way Place*. Princeton, NJ: Princeton University Press.

Index

INDEX

118